"The Object Lessons series achieves something very close to magic: the books take ordinary—even banal—objects and animate them with a rich history of invention, political struggle, science, and popular mythology. Filled with fascinating details and conveyed in sharp, accessible prose, the books make the everyday world come to life. Be warned: once you've read a few of these, you'll start walking around your house, picking up random objects, and musing aloud: 'I wonder what the story is behind this thing?'"

Steven Johnson, author of *Where Good Ideas Come From* and *How We Got to Now*

"Object Lessons describes themselves as 'short, beautiful books,' and to that, I'll say, amen. . . . If you read enough Object Lessons books, you'll fill your head with plenty of trivia to amaze and annoy your friends and loved ones—caution recommended on pontificating on the objects surrounding you. More importantly, though . . . they inspire us to take a second look at parts of the everyday that we've taken for granted. These are not so much lessons about the objects themselves, but opportunities for self-reflection and storytelling. They remind us that we are surrounded by a wondrous world, as long as we care to look.'"

John Warner, *The Chicago Tribune*

" The joy of the series . . . lies in encountering the various turns through which each of their authors has been put by his or her object. The object predominates, sits squarely center stage, directs the action. The object decides the genre, the chronology, and the limits of the study. Accordingly, the author has to take her cue from the *thing* she chose or that chose her. The result is a wonderfully uneven series of books, each one a *thing* unto itself."

Julian Yates, *Los Angeles Review of Books*

" . . . edifying and entertaining . . . perfect for slipping in a pocket and pulling out when life is on hold."

Sarah Murdoch, *Toronto Star*

" . . . a sensibility somewhere between Roland Barthes and Wes Anderson."

Simon Reynolds, author of *Retromania: Pop Culture's Addiction to Its Own Past*

OBJECTLESSONS

A book series about the hidden lives of ordinary things.

Series Editors:

Ian Bogost and Christopher Schaberg

Advisory Board:

In association with

Georgia Tech | Center for Media Studies

BOOKS IN THE SERIES

doctor

ANDREW BOMBACK

BLOOMSBURY ACADEMIC
NEW YORK • LONDON • OXFORD • NEW DELHI • SYDNEY

BLOOMSBURY ACADEMIC
Bloomsbury Publishing Inc
1385 Broadway, New York, NY 10018, USA
50 Bedford Square, London, WC1B 3DP, UK

BLOOMSBURY, BLOOMSBURY ACADEMIC and the Diana logo
are trademarks of Bloomsbury Publishing Plc

First published in the United States of America 2019

For legal purpose the Acknowledgments on p. 145 constitute an
extension of this copyright page.

Cover design: Alice Marwick

A catalog record for this book is available from the Library of Congress.

ISBN: PB: 978-1-5013-3817-5
        ePDF: 978-1-5013-3819-9
        eBook: 978-1-5013-3818-2

Series: Object Lessons

Typeset by Deanta Global Publishing Services, Chennai, India
Printed and bound in the United States of America

To find out more about our authors and books visit www.bloomsbury.com
and sign up for our newsletters.

For my father, the best doctor I'll ever know

George: When I asked him if it was cancer, he didn't give me a "get outta here." That's what I wanted to hear. "Cancer? Get outta here!"

Jerry: Well, maybe he doesn't have a "get outta here" kind of personality.

George: How could you be a doctor and not say "get outta here?" It should be part of the training at medical school. "Cancer? Get outta here! Go home! What are you, crazy? It's a little test. It's nothing. You're a real nut. You know that?"

—*SEINFELD*, "THE PILOT (PART ONE)"

CONTENTS

AUTHOR'S NOTE

To protect patient and doctor confidentiality, names and identifying details throughout this book have been changed, with the sole exception of members of my family.

INTRODUCTION

I took a week off after my son, Mateo, was born. Xenia and I kept our three-year-old daughter, Juno, home from daycare that week, too. On the morning of my first day back at work, Juno watched me making lunches for the two of us and asked why I had to go back to work. "*Porque yo soy un doctor,*" I said. "*Y tengo que ayudar los enfermos.*" I spoke to her in Spanish because Xenia is Mexican-American and we're raising our children to be bilingual. I'd been learning the language since Juno's birth via her children's books, songs, and television shows. When my Spanish-speaking patients complimented me on how much better I was handling the language, I joked that I still spoke Spanish like a three-year-old. My answer that morning might have been more nuanced and, therefore, more accurate if I'd used English.

Juno's question of why I had to go back to work was a three-year-old's way of dancing around her real question: "What, exactly, do you do when you leave our house and our family for ten hours each day?" Answering that I'm a doctor and I help the sick wasn't even an original answer. Again, I deflect some of the blame to my limited Spanish. Juno had a set of sixty Spanish flashcards called "*¿Quien?*"—thirty with a *Quien* question, and thirty with their corresponding answers. She'd throw all sixty on the floor and try to match the correct question and answer. When she brought her proposed matches to me, I'd read the cards aloud to her and say "*buen trabajo*" if she got the right pair. One pair read: "*¿Quien ayuda a la gente cuando estan enfermos?*" "*La doctora.*" That morning, as I made matching almond butter and jelly sandwiches for Juno and me, I was reciting the script from a children's game.

I might not have fared much better even if I'd answered in English. When neighbors, whose children are pre-med or are thinking about doing pre-med, ask Xenia and me about our careers, we say doctors never have to worry about finding a job, because there will always be sick people. We say the money is good and reliable. We warn that it's not as lucrative as most people think, but, still, the money allows for a more-than-comfortable life. We add that doctoring can now be lifestyle-friendly. Xenia works in shifts and often blocks off an entire week to spend time with our children. I boast about only having to work five weekends a year. Sometimes, almost as an afterthought, one of us will say it's a privilege to have a job that pays well and still provides some semblance of satisfaction that we're able to help people. Sometimes one of us uses the phrase "do some good," and the other will feel guilty about not saying this earlier.

I should have no doubt about what a doctor is meant to be, because my father is a pediatrician with an enormous practice. My brothers and I never had to wonder what my father did when he left the house. At least once a year the four of us were patients in that office and saw firsthand how well he played the role of doctor, and this role extended beyond his clinic. Every time we ate out as a family during my childhood, people would come over to our table to say hello to him. Mothers, fathers, children—they all would come over to our table at some point to say hi and show him how well they were doing. My father would smile and say how happy he was to see them. He didn't seem to relish his position, his power, his prestige, but my brothers and I did. When I was five, my father told me he was essentially immune to infections because of all the sick children he saw. I believed him. I thought he had superpowers. I thought all doctors had superpowers.

The script from Juno's *¿Quien?* flashcards would be entirely correct for my father to read if his Spanish were passable (it's not). He practices medicine as if his only task is to "help people when they're sick." Unfortunately, that mission statement feels truthful for me on some but not all days. It's probably better for Juno only to know the kind of doctor I am on some days. It might be better for patients of all ages only to know that side of doctoring. When I lived in Greece for a year between college and medical school, I made extra money giving private English lessons to an elderly couple. We sat in their living room, an hour at a time, making small talk over Johnny Walker Red and salted peanuts. They were planning a trip to Canada, for their nephew's wedding, and then some sightseeing after the wedding. They wanted to work on their English in anticipation of the trip. They had no children, but they adored their cat, Iatros. I asked about the origin of his name. "It means doctor," the husband said. "Yes," I said, "but why did you name your cat Doctor?" The wife, whose English was stronger than the husband's, said, "Cats are supposed to improve your health." "To make me better," the husband chimed in through a mouthful of peanuts.

My hospital puts out a monthly newsletter that, in truth, is an advertisement. When the newsletter focused on the nephrology division, my colleagues and I were asked to define the art of medicine. My answer was published: "For any patient who is referred here, one of our initial branching points is, 'Does this patient need to be treated?' It's a major decision whether or not to put patients on strong medicine with a number of potential toxicities. Once we've made that decision, then there are a number of therapies that we have to choose from. This is what I'd call the 'art' of what we can do here. We take these very powerful therapies and tailor them to individual patient circumstances." When I see my words in print, they look forced and deliberate. I'd have had a much easier time answering questions about the artifice of medicine. My quote in the newsletter is an example of such artifice, of touting promises that may be impossible to keep, of furthering the mythology of doctors. I'm a communicator more than a healer.

Doctor comes from the Latin *doctor*, teacher, which in turn comes from *docere*, to teach. A doctor is expected to teach his or her patients what is ailing them and what will help them get over such ailments. Every fall, I read applications for medical school, residency, and fellowship positions. Many personal statements invoke the etymology of "doctor," but virtually all do so in the context of describing a career in which the applicant teaches future physicians through an academic appointment.

The best answer to Juno's question that morning, one that admittedly wouldn't suit a child's set of flashcards, is that my job is primarily to talk. I talk to patients. I talk to patients' families. I talk to other doctors. I talk to nurses and secretaries and research technicians and insurance representatives. Sometimes I write—journal articles, grant applications, patient notes, letters to insurance companies— but that writing is another way of talking. And it's only when all of this talking approaches teaching, in that Latin sense, when I effectively communicate with patients and know that they leave my office understanding what I want (what I *need*) them to understand, that I feel like a doctor "who helps people when they're sick," as the *¿Quien?* cards prescribe.

So much of medicine seems to fall short of that ideal. Instead, the dialogues suffer from the same kind of miscommunication that Juno and I often experienced, in which I wanted to say something but needed to figure out the right way to say it. I was being so deliberate in the way I was speaking to my daughter, never feeling as if I was using my own, true language, and this may be why, at work, I'd become so attuned to the disconnect between doctors and patients.

On the drive to daycare, Juno asked me why there were so many cars on the road. "*Todos van a la estacion del tren*," I answered in Spanish to her English question. She was now old enough, and spoke Spanish well enough, to tire easily of my attempts at speaking a foreign language, so she typically saved her Spanish for her native-speaking mother and talked to me in English or, more often, Spanglish.

"They're going to the *ciudad*?" she asked.

"*Si*," I answered, "*y tu* daddy *tambien, despues* I drop you off." I looked at her reflection in the rearview mirror, waiting for her dark brown eyes to lock with mine so I could smile at her. She was clutching Patito, her beloved duck blankie, to her chest.

"You work in the *ciudad*?" she asked rhetorically. Not expecting an answer to that question, she followed up with a more difficult one: "What do you do to the *enfermos*?"

1 THE FOURTH WALL

In medical school, during my surgery rotation, I was expected to report for service rounds at 5:00 a.m. All of the patients on the floors needed to be rounded on prior to the OR cases, which began at 7:00 a.m. Therefore, to pre-round on my patients, I arrived at the hospital at 4:00 a.m. I figured this was a good time to experiment with growing out my hair and not shaving. Midway through the rotation, a cardiothoracic surgeon suggested I get a haircut and shave. He did this in private; it was not a rebuke, rather a suggestion. He advised, "Your patients want you to look and talk like the doctors on television." He was tall and trim and had perfect hair and teeth. He spoke slowly with a regal South African accent.

For the most part, I've followed his advice to this day. Every once in a while, I break the fourth wall and let the patients know I am as frustrated and disappointed with the medical system as they are. Usually, this is when they see me on the phone with an insurance company or witness my struggle in trying to obtain their medical records from another hospital.

My father, who just turned seventy, intuitively plays the part of the iconic television doctor. He defines himself as a doctor. He's been a pediatrician for over forty years; many of his patients are the children of his former patients, and some now are even the grandchildren of his former patients. When kids dress up as a doctor for Halloween, my father is the kind of doctor they are simulating. Indeed, a number of children have specifically dressed up as Dr. Bomback for Halloween. A local magazine, which profiled him as the top pediatrician in the county, asked him to pose for the cover of that issue. He and one of his patients re-created a Norman Rockwell *Saturday Evening Post* cover, my father cast as the reliable family doctor about to give a shot into a boy's rear end.

It's a morbid but entirely true thought: my father's obituary will mention his doctoring in the first sentence. That first sentence of my father's obituary—after labeling him as a husband, father, and grandfather—will say he was a devoted pediatrician to tens of thousands of children. If asked for input, I will also suggest the phrase "master diagnostician" be used. My father did a fellowship in genetics but has never used that training in his practice. He's a general pediatrician, without a true subspecialty, although websites and magazines have given him a subspecialty distinction of "difficult diagnoses." The obituary should say, "When other pediatricians needed help, their first call was to Dr. Bomback." My father was Dr. House before Dr. House existed, except my father is kind, humble, and needs sixty seconds (and not an entire TV episode's worth of drama) to make the diagnosis.

The obituary won't mention his stutter—it would be an odd detail to include in an obituary, I concede—but it should. My father does not stutter the way people stutter in movies. He doesn't repeat a consonant over and over again. His stutter is more accurately labeled a block. He blocks on words. He can't get started. He produces the sound of someone trying to clear snot from his nose without the aid of a tissue. This happens every time he answers the phone. This happens even when he is the one placing the call. "Mmmmmpphhh. Mmmmmppppphhh." A pause, then: "Hello." When he's on service, returning calls from patients (more accurately, the parents of patients) is a process. He starts his speech while dialing, hoping the block ends while the phone is ringing. He's worked with a speech therapist for years, practicing a way to essentially cough out a greeting when he calls his patients.

The doctors in movies and on television don't stutter. The best on-screen doctors see a patient, make a diagnosis immediately, and then calmly and fluently communicate their recommendations to the patients and/or their families. Think George Clooney in *ER*. Think Jerry Orbach in *Dirty Dancing*. Think Patrick Dempsey ("McDreamy") in *Grey's Anatomy*. My father knows exactly what will help the patient, knows exactly what he wants to say to the patient's parents, and then can fall into a block that looks like dry heaving. I've shadowed him in clinic and seen this happen. The parents wait for him to get out the words. They are patient, because they know his reputation; they've often traveled far distances and endured long wait times to listen to his expertise. These moments only bear the slightest embarrassment for them, but I know, because my father's told me, that these blocks are excruciating for him.

I haven't quite figured out my feelings about my father's inevitable, upcoming retirement from medicine. I should say that he hasn't decided to retire. He claims he doesn't want to retire. He just turned seventy and always pictured himself practicing into his eighties, but the moment of reckoning is fast approaching. He is virtually computer illiterate. He's lost with the electronic medical record. Two or three times a year, he asks me to help him complete an online training course required by the hospital. "I can't do this," he laments. Because his quick, illegible handwritten notes are now considered insufficient documentation, he's had to cut down his daily patient panel almost in half. He's never had to think about billing, about collecting, about the financial part of his practice. In contrast, his junior partners are de facto experts on medical economics. When the partners sold their practice this past year to a large, multispecialty medical group buying up independent practices, my father was the only one not involved in the negotiations.

My father doesn't need to work from a financial standpoint, but he is struggling with the idea of life as a non-practicing physician. His only hobby is exercising at the gym, but he mostly goes to keep my mother company. On vacation, he brings medical journals as his pleasure reading. For as long as I can remember, the magazine rack in my parents' bathroom has been stuffed with my mother's *New York* magazines and his latest copy of *Pediatric Infectious Diseases*. A retired medical school librarian, whom I cared for in the hospital, asked me if I was related to my father after I introduced myself. She told me she used to hold tapes of medical textbooks for him at the circulation desk. I remember these tapes in his car. He listened to them driving to and from work. "Your father used to thank me so much for holding the tapes for him," the librarian said, "and I didn't have the heart to tell him that no one *ever* checked them out except him."

"I waste so much time on the computer," my father tells me repeatedly, with the subtext that he's spending less time with patients and their parents. He used to brag, when he'd come home at night, about how many children he'd seen that day, sometimes fifty, sometimes sixty. He used to take pride in how he could see four children in the time a junior colleague could see one. He will be miserable when he retires, because he has always taken tremendous satisfaction from his job, but he is miserable now, because that satisfaction is slowly being taken away from him. His doctoring skills—his ability to diagnose, treat, counsel, and so on—remain unparalleled, but he has no skill in navigating what doctors of my generation call "the system." This, I surmise, is because there was no system when he started practicing. He will be relieved when he no longer has to force his outstanding but antiquated method of medicine into the modern mold of being a doctor.

The irony, of course, is that this modern style of doctoring involves less speech and, therefore, fewer opportunities for stuttering. The modern doctor "talks" with computer notes. We don't have time for thirty-minute discussions. We write our notes, and the medical records software generates a patient letter out of the note, replete with spell-check. If my father started medicine today, his stutter would be less of a handicap. Still, he'd rather struggle with his tongue than with a computer. He'd rather try to talk to patients than try to figure out which check boxes he needs to click. "It's not doctoring," he's said about electronic documentation.

The older generation of doctors—the ones my father's age—are much more confident in their abilities than my peers, and I don't think this is solely due to experience. They began their careers in an era when doctors were held in much higher esteem than they are now, and I think they bought into the collective philosophy of doctor knows best. In other words, they naturally—without any hesitation or forethought—act like on-screen doctors. My generation of doctors has doubts and realistic expectations. We were explicitly trained to avoid paternalism with our patients. It is exceedingly rare to find an ultra-cocky, young doctor in my hospital, although the type still appears on television shows and in films. He or she sticks out like a sore thumb and is roundly criticized as "overconfident," "reckless," or a "cowboy." Overconfident is a buzzword in our evaluations of the residents and fellows, a way to signal that this doctor is capable of hurting a patient.

Tom Cruise plays an overconfident doctor in *Eyes Wide Shut*. I saw this movie while in medical school, and I was intrigued by how Cruise's character flashes his medical license the way cops whip out their badges. His ability to prove he's a doctor gets him out of jams, gets him invited inside apartment buildings, gains trust from others, and makes him sexier to women. I've never seen any doctor do that—in life or in other movies—but for a while I carried my medical license in my wallet. On a plane once, a passenger was short of breath, and the flight attendants asked if there were any doctors on board who could assist. I volunteered and flashed my medical license to an unimpressed stewardess, who didn't even glance at the document.

Jordan Grumet, an internal medicine physician, performed an "autopsy" of the medical profession in a blog post entitled, "Are we witnessing the death of the modern-day physician?"[1] Grumet eulogizes the dying profession: "While some physicians are committing suicide or becoming addicted to drugs, others are leaving in less-devastating but still consequential manners: early retirement and nonclinical career paths." He then searches for "intrinsic" and "extrinsic" causes of this death.

The extrinsic factors are the predictable complaints: higher costs of education, lower salaries, less respect in the community, mountains of paperwork in a system that favors compliance over competence. I am more interested in what he calls the intrinsic cause, which is essentially the practice of medicine itself not living up to the expectations of medical students and residents. "The highs are much less common, and the lows are part of our moment-to-moment experience," Grumet writes. "Unlike most sitcoms, our patients die frequently. Diseases rarely follow patterns and rules. We lose many more battles than we win." Because I grew up with a physician father, my idea of a doctor wasn't based on someone from television or in a movie. I should not feel betrayed by medicine, that the field promised one thing and then delivered something else. Except my father's doctoring, with the sole exception of his stutter, has always been as exalted as anything on screen.

A survey of patients asked what bothered them most in a doctor's appearance. Answer choices included earrings and long hair on men, nose rings and buzz cuts on women, tattoos, bad teeth, obesity, and body odor, but the winner (or loser, I should say) was sneakers.[2] Patients did not want their doctors wearing sneakers. Doogie Howser, M.D. famously wore sneakers on the hospital wards, but what patient wants a teenager as a doctor?

A Google Images search for "doctor" reveals essentially the same picture: a doctor wearing a crisply ironed white coat with a stethoscope draped, scarf-like, around the neck. The only difference between the images is the actual doctor—man or woman; white or black or Asian. The stethoscope sits like a fashion accessory on all of them, ear pieces over one shoulder, chest piece over the other. I never saw doctors wear their stethoscopes like this until shows like *ER* and *Scrubs*.

The older doctors in my hospital, like my father, never wear their stethoscopes like this. They have the ear pieces meet at the back of the neck, like the clasps of a necklace. They project the notion they were just using the stethoscope and can use it again at a moment's notice. The "doctor" images that Google returns with the stethoscope worn in this fashion are almost exclusively cartoons, and the cartoon doctor is an old, white man, like my father.

My most obvious example of breaking the fourth wall is with my patient, Louise. She has a rare form of kidney disease, fibrillary glomerulonephritis, about which we know very little. And because we know so little about its etiology, we subsequently know even less about effective treatments. She presented with moderate kidney failure, and, in the first year of treating her, she advanced to severe kidney failure. We had tried the only therapy that had been shown in case reports to work for her disease: a monoclonal antibody called rituximab, although the rationale for why this drug would work for this specific disease was at best speculative. She broke down in my office. She was in near hysterics. Two medical students were shadowing me that day, and her crying was clearly making them uncomfortable. I handed Louise a box of tissues and told her we would re-dose the rituximab and a second round of therapy would help. I said, "You will get better," which was not an outright lie, because if her kidneys failed, she'd get a transplant, in which case she would technically get better. Louise stopped crying. "You really think so?" she said. "Yes," I said, in my most television-doctor certainty.

Later, when Louise left the office, the medical students asked me if I really thought she'd get better. "No," I said, "but she needs to have some hope right now." They laughed, but Louise did get better. After it was clear her recovery was going to be sustained, when she was stable and healthy and no longer suffering from kidney failure for over two years, I reminded Louise about that episode in my office, about her crying and my saying she would get better. She remembered it as clearly as I did. "I was bluffing," I confessed with an awkward smile, but also in a way a television doctor might say the line.

My father called me late on a Friday night. He was in a panic about an online training course required by the hospital. He couldn't get the course started. "The computer is saying something about cookies," he said timidly. "And it needs to know what version of Internet Explorer I'm using. How do I do this?"

I answered, "Maybe you should retire."

"Just help me," my father said. "Please."

The exchange felt like something on television.

2 MY FAVORITE TYPES OF PATIENTS

My favorite types of patients (in descending order): once sick but now healthy and attributes his or her good health to my care; sick, seeing me for the first time, and optimistic that my recommendations will help; sick, following my recommendations, and understands that I am trying my best to help, but there is a limit to what medicine can do; sick, following my recommendations, and questions why he or she is not getting better; sick, not following my recommendations, but now will consider following my recommendations; sick, not following my recommendations, and has his or her own ideas on how to proceed based on what he or she has learned on the internet; healthy, never sick, never really needed to see me, and appreciative of that good health; healthy, never sick, never really needed to see me, but convinced that there is something wrong that I have yet to find.

There's a major disconnect between what patients expect of their doctors and what doctors are actually able to do. The other day I walked past a urologist, standing outside an operating room, talking to a patient's wife. I was able to hear the urologist tell the wife he'd removed a large kidney stone: the husband would be fine now as long as he drank plenty of fluids to prevent another stone. The urologist had a great head of silver hair and looked a lot like Richard Gere. His smile expressed pure contentment that he'd done the right thing. The wife was looking up at him with an equally content expression that she and her husband had gotten everything out of the doctor they'd wanted.

As I left them behind to finish up their conversation, I thought how this scene is so much the exception rather than the norm, yet it's the scene we doctors want to play, and the scene our patients want to play along with us, too. The next time I saw this Richard Gere-looking urologist, he was standing by an elevator, nervously running his hand through his magnificent silver hair, talking on his cell phone and telling someone he'd be there as fast as he could. The smile was gone.

Last year, a medical student was hospitalized with a mysterious illness, and no one in our hospital was able to make a diagnosis for her and her family. She grew sicker and sicker each day, and eventually she died despite having dozens of our best physicians on her case. Her classmates were devastated, as much by the loss of their friend as by watching their teachers fail. "Those attendings were our heroes," a student told me. I'd asked him about a pin he was wearing on his white coat. It turned out the pin was a way to commemorate his former classmate. "We thought they were geniuses, that they knew everything. I mean, we'd really only been exposed to them in the classroom, but it felt like there was nothing they didn't know. That was one of the worst parts of watching her die. Every time a new attending came onto the case, we'd all be like, 'Okay, well now Dr. A—will figure it out, or now Dr. G—will figure it out,' but no one did."

Harold Roberts, whose research helped decode the clotting cascade (the series of proteins in our bodies that prevent us from bleeding out), was an emeritus professor at the University of North Carolina when I was a resident in internal medicine. He gave grand rounds about his discovery, many years earlier, of a crucial clotting factor. His lecture relayed the story of the patient, a young boy, whose genetic predisposition to bleeding keyed Roberts into his breakthrough finding. When the boy died, his mother asked if Roberts and his colleagues could attend the funeral wearing their white coats. Roberts, nearing age ninety, confessed that he'd viewed the boy and his mother as more than just a patient and his family, and her request unsettled him. The boy and his mother had viewed Roberts solely as a doctor, and now he was the doctor of a boy whose life he was unable to save.

Drs. Tammy Hoffmann and Chris Del Mar systematically reviewed all studies that have quantitatively assessed patients' expectations of the benefits and harms of any treatment, diagnostic test, or screening test. In their review of 35 studies with over 27,000 patients, they reported that the majority of patients overestimated intervention benefit and underestimated harm. In the conclusion of their systematic review, Drs. Hoffman and Del Mar used pointed language almost never seen in a scientific article: "The importance of this review's findings relates to the appetite that people have for medical interventions. Many want to have more and resist having less. Unless this is countered by accurate and balanced information, it will continue to be a driver for more intervention use than benefits society."[1]

This kind of commentary would be expected in an editorial accompanying the article. In fact, Dr. Deborah Korenstein in a companion editorial said, "The systematic tendency for patients to misunderstand benefits and harms is a fundamental threat to our ability to improve health care value and must be addressed."[2] I can only presume the peer reviewers and the journal editors felt so aligned with Drs. Hoffman and Del Mar that they allowed their grandstanding conclusion. They, too, felt that doctors were under attack by uninformed patients who want more, more, more.

On January 20, 2015, Dr. Michael Davidson, a forty-four-year-old cardiovascular surgeon, was shot twice in his office at the Brigham & Women's Hospital in Boston. He died a few hours later. Stephen Pasceri, the man who murdered Dr. Davidson and then killed himself in an exam room, was apparently frustrated with the American health care system. When his father died in 2011, he publicly asked then-Massachusetts Senator John Kerry to conduct an investigation into his father's exorbitant medical bills. His mother, a patient of Dr. Davidson's, died two months before the Brigham shooting.

A few weeks after the murder, the *Boston Globe* published a detailed account of the events before, during, and after the fateful shooting.[3] Stephen Pasceri's mother, Marguerite, underwent heart valve surgery at the Brigham. Dr. Davidson, a surgeon known to operate on the sickest and riskiest patients, like Marguerite, was one of the few surgeons who would have taken her case. There were complications post-operatively, including the development of a dysrhythmia and the use of the anti-arrhythmic drug, amiodarone. Eventually, Marguerite's family, in accordance with her pre-stated wishes, took her off life support The cause of death on her death certificate was "cardiovascular collapse," the culmination of her many pre-existing co-morbidities. Her son, Stephen, felt that amiodarone was responsible for her decline based on what he'd read online about its toxicities. Before heading off to murder Dr. Davidson, he left a thumb drive filled with his final thoughts in an envelope addressed to his brother. The thumb drive files laid out his "research" on amiodarone and his certainty that Dr. Davidson was responsible for his mother's death.

On January 20, 2015, Stephen Pasceri idled around the Brigham for an hour—he bought a bottle of water and a newspaper from the Au Bon Pain in the hospital lobby—

before heading to Dr. Davidson's clinic. "I want to see Dr. Davidson," he said to the secretary. "I've traveled a long way. I have to see Dr. Davidson. I'm not leaving without seeing him." At first, Dr. Davidson offered to meet with Pasceri in the afternoon, after his clinic, so he would have ample time. But Pasceri was adamant, and Dr. Davidson was accommodating. Pasceri was led back to an exam room. Dr. Davidson's physician assistant was with him at the beginning of the encounter, and she reported that Pasceri asked Dr. Davidson to open the internet, go to drugs.com, and look up amiodarone. "Are you aware that this drug is extremely toxic?" Pasceri asked, pointing to the computer. "Do you see all of the warnings on drugs.com?"

Eventually, Dr. Davidson asked his assistant to leave the room and start seeing other patients, so the clinic wouldn't fall too far behind schedule. He remained in the room with Stephen Pasceri for twenty-five more minutes before shots were heard. In those twenty-five minutes, I suspect Dr. Davidson tried to console the son for the loss of his mother, tried to explain how frequently he and other doctors (doctors like me) prescribe amiodarone, tried to convince this man that he had helped his mother, or at least tried to, and that he needed to move on to other patients who needed similar help. That's what I would have done. I would have talked and talked and talked.

Michael Davidson was six years older than me. Like me, he was married to another doctor. He had three young children and his wife was pregnant with their fourth child when he was murdered. His wife told the *Globe,* "My children asked why this man killed Daddy when he got to have his mother his whole life and they only had their Daddy for a short time. Sometimes the most brilliant questions come out of the mouths of babes."

I did not seek out articles about Michael Davidson. Everything I learned about his murder came from articles that were posted on Facebook by doctor friends. These friends almost never post on Facebook. When they do, it's to share pictures of their children or their pets. Yet now they were posting articles, day after day, about the murder. This was how we communicated our sadness and anger, through links to newspaper articles. My friends, like me, mourned the doctor's death but also were furious with the circumstances leading up to the death.

The *Globe* article was accompanied by screenshots of the Brigham's surveillance video from the morning of the murder. We see Stephen Pasceri walking throughout the hospital in the hour before he confronted Dr. Davidson. I'm sure it's because I know what this man did—what would happen after these surveillance videos were shot—that makes me see these photos and hate the entitled look on his face. It's a look of someone who thinks he knows more about medicine than the doctor he murdered.

I get nervous when the labs from my sickest patients come through the fax machine, or when I load them up on my computer screen, wondering just how bad they'll be this time. Sometimes, when I catch myself being nervous, when I realize my heart is racing, I remind myself that the patients experience much more anxiety when I relay these lab results. This is similar to what Sallie Tisdale, a writer who's also worked as an oncology nurse, confesses in her essay, "Twitchy": "I am periodically reminded by my patients that what is normal to me (the sounds, the smells) is a strange and frightening world to them."[4]

On a Friday afternoon, just before leaving work, I picked up messages from my secretary. One of the messages was from a patient, sick with a cold, who wanted antibiotics called into her local pharmacy. If it was any time other than Friday afternoon at 5:00 p.m., I would have called her instead of the pharmacy. I'd probably have elicited symptoms more consistent with a viral infection than a bacterial infection. I'd probably have said that antibiotics won't help, that all she needed was rest and hydration. She just as likely would have disagreed or, in the very least, felt disappointed in not having the security of antibiotics for the weekend. Maybe she's a fan of another writer, Dodie Bellamy, who said (joked?) in *When the Sick Rule the World*, "There is no such thing as a hypochondriac; there are only doctors who cannot figure out what is wrong with you."[5]

All of this is my way of explaining why I called the pharmacy, rather than the patient, from my cell phone on the way home. I can rationalize that it was my way of empathizing with my patient, of understanding her "strange and frightening world" of feeling sick, but I can just as easily admit I took the easiest route and felt a great sense of disappointment, even though the patient, I'm sure, was thrilled with the results. My father, I should note, has a reputation for not prescribing antibiotics for earaches and sore throats. Other doctors laud him for this practice, as do many parents. Some, though, switch pediatricians. These are often young parents with their first child.

Another patient, a lawyer, emailed me to find out his latest test results. I relayed the numbers and then gave a brief, one-sentence editorial: "These are excellent results, so let's just plan on repeating them in three months to see if they remain this good."

He emailed me back: "What do these current labs say about my long-term prognosis?"

I responded: "They say that everything looks good now, but only a series of similarly good labs, over a significant period of time, can give a reasonable prediction of your prognosis."

He replied: "So, in retrospect, would you say that the email you sent me three months ago was premature or overly optimistic?" He sent this last email as a reply to an email I'd sent about his labs three months earlier. I reread that old email and could see how his lawyerly mind might have locked onto one phrase in my email: "If the labs look this good in three months, that's a good prognostic sign."

I replied: "The message in that email is the same as in the email I sent regarding these recent labs—every subsequent set of labs that are good increases your chances of a good long-term prognosis. But nothing beats time. My hope is that we're sending nearly identical emails one, two, three years from now."

He didn't respond.

Mateo was born in the triage bay of my hospital's birthing floor. We'd arrived about four hours before Xenia was ready to push, but all fifteen labor and delivery beds were filled. The nurses kept reassuring us we'd get a room, and Xenia kept predicting she'd be forced to give birth on a triage stretcher. When her contractions were less than a minute apart, the nurse told us the delivery would have to occur in triage. "It's not a good space to have a baby," she said. She knew we were both doctors, so that's probably why she was so honest with us. Then she said, "All the doctors are tied up in an emergency C-section, so I had to page another doctor to come from clinic."

The obstetrician, whom we'd never seen before, arrived five minutes later, put on gloves, examined Xenia, and told the nurse to open the crash cart. I looked at her name tag—Dr. Peralta—because I knew I'd be telling this story again and again and again. Dr. Peralta remained perfectly calm as she coached Xenia and ushered Mateo out in about three minutes. She handed him over to Xenia, called her "mommy" and congratulated both of us, then promptly disappeared as soon as an intern showed up to take care of the afterbirth. Later, we'd talk about Dr. Peralta as if she were a superhero, how she swooped in at the last moment, took care of everything, and vanished before we had a chance to properly thank her.

A few weeks later, I saw her in an elevator at work. She, of course, didn't recognize me, but that just added to my excitement in seeing her again. I couldn't wait to tell Xenia I'd been on the elevator with Dr. Peralta. But just as I got up the nerve to speak to her, she started talking to a colleague about an awful first date she'd just had, about how the guy had much less hair than in his online profile, and how the restaurant he'd chosen was in a bad neighborhood. I didn't want to hear this conversation. I was being unfair to her, wanting her only to exist as she did in my mind, as the doctor who'd effortlessly delivered my son amidst the disaster area of triage bay. I wanted her to be a superhero, and she just wanted to be another person in the elevator.

3 I HAVE GOOD NEWS AND BAD NEWS

A man sees a doctor for help with a debilitating stutter. After a thorough examination, the doctor relays his diagnosis. "Your penis is too long, by about five inches," the doctor explains. "It's dragging down your abdomen, including your diaphragm, and making you stutter. If we remove five inches from your penis, the stutter should go away." The patient answers, "I-I-I-I-I'll d-d-d-do a-a-a-a-a-any-th-th-th-ing." Four weeks after successful surgery, the patient returns to the doctor's office. "My speech is great," he says fluently, "and I haven't had a single stutter since the surgery. But the problem is I've completely lost my libido. I can't go on like this. Even if it means I have to stutter, I'd like you to reattach the five inches back to my penis." The doctor replies, "F-f-f-f-f-f-fuck y-y-y-y-ou!"

Doctors love doctor jokes. We trade them over email. We start our lectures with them. We'll interrupt them to supply the punch line and prove that we've heard them before. At my medical school graduation, the keynote speaker opened with a joke: "You start medical school saying, 'I don't know.' Now, as a fellow physician, please join me in saying, 'We don't know.'"

But doctors almost never tell doctor jokes in front of patients, because doctor jokes follow patterns, and the most common model is the "the doctor is an asshole" joke. The asshole emerges not in the doctor's actions but in the way the doctor speaks, in the words he says to his patients.

A man is in the hospital with two broken legs. The doctor comes in and says, "I have good news and bad news." The man asks for the bad news first. The doctor says, "We're going to have to remove your legs." Then the man asks for the good news. The doctor says, "The guy in the next bed wants to buy your sneakers."

Or a doctor tells his patient she has terminal cancer. "Terminal?" she asks. "As in, there's nothing you can do about it?" "Nothing," the doctor says, "nothing at all." "Well, with all due respect," the patient counters, "I want a second opinion." "Okay," the doctor says, "you're ugly, too."

Another pattern of doctor jokes is the "the poor patient doesn't even know how bad his or her plight really is" joke. In these jokes, there is either an overt or implied statement about the treating doctor's lack of empathy. So, in essence, those doctor jokes are also "the doctor is an asshole" jokes. A doctor says to an old man, "You've got cancer and

Alzheimer's disease." And the old man says, "Thank God I don't have cancer."

I wish I could say this kind of humor is limited solely to such open-mic-level jokes. But sometimes, at least for me, doctor jokes seep into my practice. I have a patient with a congenital disorder that led to both kidney failure and blindness. She sees me twice a year. She often talks excitedly about her boyfriend. She is morbidly obese and, in my darker moments, I've thought about what kind of guy would date her. I've thought of Jerry Seinfeld or Larry David (more precisely, the characters of themselves in their shows) saying, "You're supposed to get an automatic upgrade when you date a blind woman. If she's his version of an upgrade, can you imagine the specimen *he* is?" I was always a bit uncomfortable with the way doctors were depicted in *Seinfeld* and *Curb Your Enthusiasm*, however. Their misanthropy somehow stood out among all the other misanthropy on display.

In some jokes, the doctor and the patient are both assholes. A man told his doctor he wasn't able to do all the things around the house that he used to do. When the examination was complete, he said, "Now, Doc, I can take it. Tell me in plain English what's wrong with me." "Well, in plain English," the doctor replied, "you're just lazy." "Okay," said the man. "Now give me the medical term so I can tell my wife."

I don't feel as bad when these kinds of doctor jokes invade my clinical space. A patient of mine forced me to order an MRI of her brain given persistent headaches and her fears, based on her internet reading, that she had a brain tumor. The scan was negative. My secretary told me she called to discuss her results. I pretended to pick up the phone and call her, joking for my secretary, "The MRI of your brain is back and the results say you are fucking crazy. I've never seen them curse in their reports before, but here it is. The official radiology report says, 'You are fucking crazy.'"

At another time, about the same patient, who calls all the time and reschedules her appointments at the last minute and often needs to be squeezed in or added onto the schedule, I said to my secretary, "She thinks she's a V.I.P. but she's really a V.A.P.—a very annoying person." So now we just refer to her as the V.A.P.

On my first night on-call as an intern, I admitted a hemophiliac on a Friday who died by Sunday of an intracerebral hemorrhage. He'd presented to the emergency room that Friday night complaining of a headache and severe constipation. He was given an enema and sent for a head CT. The next morning, presenting his case to my team, I explained my working theory that the intracerebral bleeding was caused, at least in part, by excessive straining to move his bowels. He'd burst a blood vessel trying to defecate. My first patient death may have been prevented by a stool softener, by laxatives, by prunes.

Within a week, I was telling this story as a joke to my co-interns. None of us was more than a month removed from our medical school graduations, but we all laughed. We were doctors now. Even today, if asked how my first patient died, I tell the story in a humorous light, as a real life version of a doctor joke.

While doctors tell each other doctor jokes, patients rarely tell doctor jokes. Doctors acknowledge the jokes that underlie their profession. Malcolm Gladwell, discussing why people tell jokes about themselves (his specific reference was engineers making engineering jokes), said that jokes are "grievances."[1] Jokes are a way for a group of people to complain: *This is the way we think! Why doesn't everyone else think like us?* Patients don't want to think of themselves or their doctors as punch lines. Doctors talk about themselves in the context of a joke. Patients laugh uncomfortably at these jokes. Their health isn't funny.

At age seventy-six, Sam, a retired family practitioner, received a kidney transplant from his wife just before he needed to start dialysis. Six years later, he's as healthy as any 82-year-old I know. "My wife saved my life," he says, and he's entirely right. His life expectancy on dialysis at seventy-six years of age would have been less than two years. He has a coarse tremor in both of his hands, although it's more pronounced in his right hand. "I'm pretty certain the tremor is from your Prograf," I said, relaying a common side effect of one of his anti-rejection medications. "If this were Parkinson's, I'd expect you to have some change in your walk, and usually there are some tell-tale signs in the face with Parkinson's, too. I don't see any of that. It's all just in your hands." Sam agreed. "There's some old joke," I continued, "about the guy with Parkinson's and his masturbation skills." Sam didn't laugh. Instead, he corrected me. The wife has Parkinson's in that joke.

I can't recall a doctor joke in which the doctor is a female. I asked Xenia if she knew any female doctor jokes. "A man and his son are in a horrible car accident, and the man dies immediately. The son is taken by ambulance to the nearest emergency room and the doctor says, 'This boy needs emergency surgery to save his life, but I can't do it, because—'"

"'Because he's my son,'" I interrupted her. "The ER doctor's his mom. That's a riddle, not a joke."

It's a riddle our children should have no problems solving.

For a week during my third year of medical school, I worked with my father in the pediatric emergency room. The only patient I remember from that week was a sixteen-year-old boy who came in complaining of a sore throat. He was worried he'd caught mono from his girlfriend. Like all medical students, I did a full physical exam on every patient I saw, eager to practice my abdominal percussion skills and perfect my use of the tuning fork. When I did a testicular exam on this sixteen-year-old, I thought I felt a lump.

After seeing the patient, I presented the case to my father, including my exam finding of a potential lump on his right testicle. I returned to the exam room with my father, who immediately began examining the boy's testicles. "I don't feel anything," he said after almost a minute of rubbing the boy's testicles between his fingers. "You said it was on the right?" he asked me.

"I think so," I said, "but it may have been on the left."

"Come here and show me where you felt it," my father said.

I walked over, my father let go of the boy's scrotum, and I dutifully took hold. "Hey man," the boy said, backing away from my grip. "I came in here for my throat." I started to laugh. I tried to stop myself, but that effort made me laugh even harder. I looked over at my dad, who was smiling but had already helped the boy pull up his pants with one hand and was searching his neck for swollen lymph nodes with the other hand.

I excused myself from the room and went back to the doctor's conference room to laugh in private. When my father returned a few minutes later, I was still laughing. I don't know what he would have done with any other medical student, but with me, he started laughing, too. "You can't laugh around patients," he counseled me through his own laughter. "You have to get that out of your system. You can't do that." We gave ourselves another minute to laugh, and then he sent me out to see the next patient.

I'm not sure if that story is a doctor joke, but my father and I retell it often. If it is a doctor joke, I don't know what pattern or model it fits.

4 YOU GET BETTER BECAUSE WE ARE BETTER

Hospital slogans are the opposite of doctor jokes. Doctor jokes claim to represent a fictitious world that, upon closer inspection, reflects a fair amount of what goes on between doctors and patients. Hospital slogans, on the other hand, are presented as mission statements, axioms of truth, ideals of honest doctoring. Most doctors laugh just as heartily at our hospitals' slogans as we do at doctor jokes, amused by the claims our institutions make on our behalf and how far these claims stray from the nuts-and-bolts reality of our daily routines.

In theory, hospital slogans should be a way for doctors to communicate with patients. In practice, hospitals pay advertising firms to come up with slogans. Business and advertising websites rank the best hospital slogans. Sometimes these websites use the term "taglines" instead of slogans. Doctors would never be optimistic enough to come up with the kind of language that fills these taglines and slogans. The advertisers are patients, or at least potential patients. The slogans they provide hospitals are more a statement of what patients want than what doctors can offer:

This is your healthcare.
We'll earn your trust.
Your good health is our greatest achievement.
More science, less fear.
A transforming, healing presence.
Dedicated to hope, healing, and recovery.
Changing lives.
Changing medicine, changing lives.

Bernard Lown's *The Lost Art of Healing* is billed as a memoir.[1] The book's jacket copy reads, "Drawing on four decades of practice as a cardiologist and a vast knowledge of literature and medical history, Dr. Lown probes the heart and soul of the doctor-patient relationship." *The Lost Art of Healing* is more a polemic than a memoir. Lown recalls the simple advice he received from a Siberian physician—"Every time a doctor sees a patient, the patient should feel better as a result"—and spends most of his book bemoaning how far the American medical system has strayed from this maxim.

Lown blames language. The modern physician spends much of his or her day talking to patients, but the dialogue is too sterile, too technical, or too superficial to benefit the patient. Hospital slogans suffer from the same failings.

"Every time a doctor sees a patient, the patient should feel better as a result" is the only slogan any hospital should need. Lown wants physicians to speak to their patients with heartfelt compassion: "I know of few remedies more powerful than a carefully chosen word. Patients crave caring, which is dispensed largely with words. Talk, which can be therapeutic, is one of the underrated tools in a physician's armamentarium."

I don't think Lown would consider the commanding language of hospital slogans—You get better because we are better—therapeutic talking.

A medical humor website (yes, these exist) called *Gomer Blog* ran a parody news article about "new, brutally-honest slogans" adopted by hospitals.[2] Some examples:

Death is inevitable.
Underpaid, underachieving.
Quantity, not quality.
Tired, so tired.
Compassion, innovation, et cetera.
Where billing comes first.
We're out of narcotics.

Compare those physician-penned slogans to what advertisers consider the best taglines: Home of the best ideas in medicine. The skill to heal. The spirit to care. Because your life matters. Depend on us for life. Better for you. When your child needs a hospital, everything matters. That's powerful healing. A union of compassion and healthcare. Your full circle of care. Dedication beyond measure. Bettering the human condition.

I've said these taglines to patients: We're trying our best. We're doing everything we can. Sometimes even the best medicine fails. Sometimes the best medicine is recognizing failure and stopping before more harm is done. I know it's hard.

I've never said these taglines to patients: For the journey that is life. Giving children the care they deserve. Exceptional care, exceptional people. Exceptional technology, extraordinary care. Every day, a new discovery.

BRAZOS BOOKSTORE

2421 Bissonnet Street, Houston, Texas
713-523-0701 I brazosbookstore.com
Open Mon-Sat 10am to 8pm Sun 12pm to 6pm

Find us on Facebook, Twitter & Instagram

400493 Reg 1 7:43 pm 02/10/19

S DOCTOR	1 @	14.95	14.95
S WHAT SHAPE IS SPA	1 @	18.95	18.95
S BEYOND WEIRD	1 @	26.00	26.00
SUBTOTAL			59.90
SALES TAX - 8.25%			4.94
TOTAL			64.84
DISCOVER CARD PAYMENT			64.84

"It's lit."
- Brazos Bookstore

5 DOCTORS AT HOME

Xenia and I were sitting on my parents' couch, sipping wine, while our kids were upstairs sleeping. Xenia said I was not as helpful when Mateo woke up in the middle of the night as I'd been with Juno three years earlier. "He's so grumpy about it now," Xenia said.

"Your father would jump out of bed to get you and your brothers when you cried," my mother admonished me. "He never complained, not once. He'd stay awake until I was done feeding you, and then *he'd* take you back to your crib."

I doubted the veracity of the story. As a grandfather, my father is a bit more hands off than would be expected of a pediatrician. My mother urged my father to set the record straight.

"It's true," he said. "I was so grateful to have healthy children, how could I complain about them waking up at night?"

Doctors remain doctors at home. We act like doctors with our families. We speak like doctors to our children. My generation of doctors has fought for more boundaries than my father's generation of doctors, so we don't have to bring our work home with us. We want to leave behind the sickness and the demands on our time inside the hospital's doors. Still, we enter our homes as doctors, and we remain doctors until we leave for the next shift.

When my father used to bathe me and my brothers, he would obsessively examine our bodies for black and blue marks. When he found one, he'd press to ensure the bruise hurt. He was screening us for leukemia. This was one of the ways he communicated his love to us.

I was thirty-five when Juno was born, roughly four years after Xenia and I started trying to have a baby. I constantly think about how lucky we were to have her, which immediately transforms into incessant worrying about how she could die at any moment. It's an awful fear to have because (a) Juno is healthy, and (b) I spend all of my working days around people who are not. I suspect this type of anxiety is shared by all parents, to some degree, but is particularly felt by parents who've struggled with infertility and by parents who are physicians. I unfortunately fall into that most anxious part of the Venn diagram encompassing physician parents who've struggled with infertility.

Juno woke up early, a few minutes after 5:00 a.m., and said she wasn't tired. I told her she could play quietly in her room until 6:00 a.m., and then we could have breakfast together. When I returned, she was sitting on the floor, cradling one of her dolls in her arms. The doll had a toy blood pressure cuff dangling from its bicep.

"My baby's *enferma*," Juno said.

"*Que paso*?" I asked.

"I don't know. I think her temperature's not feeling well."

I fished out the toy stethoscope from her chest of dress-up gear and sat down on the floor. I offered to listen to the doll's chest and examine her. "No, Daddy," Juno said. "*Yo soy una doctora*. I'm taking care of her." I smiled. "I'm going to give her a shot," she continued. She handed me the doll while she searched for her toy doctor's kit. After placing the plastic needle against the doll's leg, she instructed me to put the baby doll into its baby doll crib.

"My baby needs to sleep now, okay," she said. "Let's eat *desayuno*."

The next morning, Juno informed me, "My baby's still sick."

"*Todavia esta enferma?*" I asked, as much to show her that I could still speak Spanish as to relay my own, true sense of puzzlement.

She hadn't talked about or played with the doll since the previous morning's shot, which seemed to have cured everything. "*Si*," Juno said. She started to cry, and I asked her what was wrong. "*No se porque esta enferma, Daddy*." She moved in for a hug. I wiped away her tears and suggested we examine the baby together. The baby probably had an ear infection, I told her, and we could give her some medicine. My Spanish flowed easily as I relied on the medical terms I so often used with Spanish-speaking patients. "Okay, Daddy," she said, pulling herself together, shifting back into English now that she had more control of the situation. She was holding my hand and squeezed tighter as she sniffed away the last of her tears.

My mother-in-law stayed with us for two weeks after Mateo was born. She taught Juno a song to sing to her little brother. The song begins, "*Amor chiquito acabado de nacer.*" My ear for Spanish is bad; when I tried the song, I sang, "*Amor chiquito a caballo de nacer.*" My substitution of "my little love, finally born" with "my little love, a newborn horse" cracked Juno up and ruined the song for everyone in the house, because now she would only sing the version with the wrong lyrics.

"She's so impressionable," I said to Xenia.

"I don't know why that surprises you," Xenia replied. "I've told you, like a zillion times, you have to be very careful what you say around her."

When my father was on call, if we were out of the house, he'd sometimes say "shit" when his pager rang. This was before cell phones, so a page meant he'd have to locate the nearest pay phone. That stress of having to find a phone (or, even worse for a stutterer like my father, having to ask for directions to the nearest phone) was the impetus behind that "shit." My younger brother, barely two years old, once beat my dad to the "shit" when his pager interrupted our dinner at a Chinese restaurant. We all laughed. "Shit," my younger brother repeated with a smile, encouraged by his audience. "Shit. Shit. Shit." My father left the table to return the page from the Chinese restaurant's phone. The owner's two sons were patients of my father, and he was always happy to offer his phone.

In the last year, I've taken on more research and administrative work and cut down on my clinical time. This kind of time re-allotment, fairly typical for someone who stays in academics and is trying to advance to a higher professorial rank, has come at the cost (or, some might say, benefit) of seeing fewer patients. The other cost is that Juno's view of what I do has started to shift away from the idealistic view of a doctor making his sick patients healthy to the more realistic perception of an academic physician in the twenty-first century.

"I'm going to work," she said recently, driving away from me in her toy car, leaving me alone in the living room as she headed toward her bedroom-cum-office. I checked my phone for email, read a recap of the previous night's Knicks game, and then went to her room to check on her. She was talking into a toy smart phone.

"*Que estas haciendo*?" I asked.

"I'm on a conference call," she said. "Shhhh-h-h-h-h, Daddy."

On other occasions, she's substituted the word "meeting" for "work" in our conversations, as in "Do you have to go to a meeting today, Daddy?" or "I missed you when you were at your meeting." Her aunt asked her recently what she wanted to do when she grew up, and Juno answered, "Write papers."

An early reader of this chapter commented, "What your kids think about your job seems really important to you." I replied, "Isn't that the way every parent thinks?" She said, "Sure, but you'd think that would be more of an issue for someone who works in finance or advertising, not for someone who's a doctor." When I didn't immediately reply, she added, "It's interesting to me. It surprised me, to think that a doctor worried about whether his kids thought he did something meaningful."

When Xenia and I argue, she says, "You don't listen. You're so quick to propose a solution, all you want to do is fix the problem, but you have no interest in actually listening to the problem. You talk too much." She knows it's an effective jab, because the criticism extends far beyond the subject we're arguing about and pokes at my doctoring abilities. The rebuke, if placed in an entirely medical context, could crush a doctor in training.

Xenia, an internal medicine hospitalist, often voices regret she didn't go into surgery. She says, "I'd feel like I'm helping people rather than just trying to get someone out of the hospital." Surgeons talk, but they also do, and sometimes they fix. Surgeons have more job satisfaction than physicians like my wife. She knows this, but she also knows her family life would suffer if she were a surgeon. "I couldn't be the mother that I am if I went into surgery," she typically concludes. "I'd never see my kids."

"And you'd be a real bitch as a surgeon," I add.

She always agrees.

In bed, Xenia told me about one of her patients, a heroin addict admitted for bacterial endocarditis, an infection of one of her heart valves. This has been our usual pillow talk since residency, recapping the day's nightmares (never the day's successes). Doctors talk to other doctors about their work. It's our common language. Xenia and I are no different in our bedroom: we're husband and wife, but we're also two doctors swapping horror stories.

Xenia felt awful that night, because she'd had to call in the hospital's lawyers to prevent this patient from signing herself out against medical advice. "She kept pleading to me," Xenia said. "She kept saying, 'Please, please, I have to get home to be with my kids.'" Xenia took my hand under the blankets. "She was covered with track marks—both arms, the neck, legs, everywhere. And I'm listening to her and looking at her and thinking about you and me, for some reason."

"Why?" I asked.

"Because we're too hard on ourselves sometimes," she said, squeezing my hand. "We're good parents."

In medical school, I used to bristle when the residents or attendings told me they knew my father, because I felt the other, hypercompetitive students would accuse me of nepotism. My decision to leave New York and do my residency and fellowship training in North Carolina was perhaps, on a subconscious level, a decision to see if I could succeed in medicine where no one knew the Bomback name. Or maybe not. I was also leaving New York because the girl I loved didn't love me back, because I was tired of taking the subway and having a tiny apartment, and because that same girl I loved who didn't love me back told me she'd visit me in North Carolina. She never did. Still, it's important for me to know I succeeded in a hospital where no one knew my father.

Now I feel nothing but pride when someone mentions my father to me in a professional context. This could be a patient, telling me their children used to see my father. This could be another doctor, momentarily breaking from a conversation to ask about my father. Best of all is a medical student who's just rotated with my father in the pediatric emergency room and absorbed one of his legendary talks about non-legendary topics such as ear infections and diaper rashes, and who asks starry-eyed if I'm "related to Dr. Bomback." My heart skips a beat when I answer that question, because I anticipate the next sentence, some variation of "He's so great."

I used to try to get these exchanges over with quickly. I wanted the medical students to appreciate me, not him. I wanted to be their role model. Now I linger over these exchanges. I extend the conversations. "What was your favorite case with him?" I ask. "Did you see any zebras with him?" Zebras, in medical lingo, are rare diagnoses, in contrast to the more common ailments we call horses. I listen to their stories and wonder how much longer I'll have these opportunities to admire my father's work.

My father came over for lunch and to examine Mateo, whom Xenia and I had self-diagnosed with croup. We called up my father and let him hear Mateo's barking cough over the phone. He agreed with the diagnosis. "He may need steroids," my father said over the phone. "Do you hear any stridor or wheezing?" Not trusting my or Xenia's physical exam skills, he offered to come over.

"Here you go, Bampa," Juno said as he entered our home. She handed him her toy stethoscope, which is the same plastic stethoscope used in the hospital for patients on isolation. "Let Bampa eat first," I said. "No, let me examine him first," my father said, donning the stethoscope, putting in the ear pieces, gearing up like an athlete in pregame warm-ups. Juno stood by his leg and looked up in awe at her grandfather.

She wore the same look as my department chairman when he'd recently introduced our grand rounds speaker. "Usually, when I introduce a speaker," he said, "I relay the highlights of his or her very impressive CV, and I could easily do that with today's speaker. But, instead, I'd rather just say that a year ago, when my son was in the intensive care unit, I asked her to be his pulmonologist. And when a physician entrusts the care of his child to another physician—" He stopped. With his index finger, he swatted away a tear from his right eye. His voice cracked a bit when he continued. "That, to me, is the ultimate accolade."

"Is he still *enfermo*?" Juno asked about her brother after my father left.

"*Si*," I answered.

"Bampa didn't make him better?" she asked. She was wearing her plastic isolation stethoscope, the ear pieces intersecting at the back of her neck. She started swaying her shoulders back and forth so that the stethoscope's chest piece swung like a pendulum.

"He tried," I said.

At my father's advice, we created a pseudo-steam room in our bathroom for Mateo. After about fifteen minutes in the steam, we bundled him up and took him outside into the wintry air, letting the cold reduce the inflammation in his airways. He was breathing better now, and he was sleeping.

"Bampa's so nice," Juno said, still swaying and enjoying the stethoscope's dance across her chest. "He's so, so nice."

6 TEXTERS AND EMAILERS AND TWEETERS

Mateo was three weeks old, and Xenia fell into a panic at 2:30 a.m. while breastfeeding him. Balancing him on a breastfeeding pillow with her left arm, she used her right hand to read about the bright green color of his bowel movements on her phone. She jumped around from one website to another. In less than ten minutes (the time she had him on her right breast), she became convinced he was either suffering from foremilk/hindmilk imbalance or had developed an allergy to something in her diet.

"Most of the sites say it's dairy," she read off her phone.

I took Mateo and burped him while Xenia covered up her right breast and bared her left breast. We were both exhausted. She said she would call the pediatrician in the morning.

"You're acting crazy," I said. "He's eating fine. He's gaining weight. What would you say if one of your patients tried to self-diagnose off the internet at two in the morning?"

"I can call if I want to," she countered, but she didn't call.

A week later, at Mateo's regularly scheduled one-month appointment, he was diagnosed with cow's milk protein intolerance.

Many doctors now share their cell phone numbers with their patients. Some text with their patients. They communicate with their patients the same way they'd communicate with friends. I, on the other hand, always try to return patient calls from an office phone or my home phone, which has a blocked number. If I do return a call on my cell phone, I type in the two-digit code that temporarily conceals my number. On the rare occasions I've forgotten to do that, the patients invariably use my cell phone for future correspondence. It's not entirely their fault, I suppose, because they probably have their other doctors' mobile numbers. I do email with patients, although I recite a rehearsed caveat before sharing my email address. "Email is only for non-urgent matters," I say. "Any emergency has to be called in. You should assume I only check email once a day." This last sentence couldn't be further from the truth, as I check email at least ten times an hour.

My favorite patient email used the subject heading, "Size of a baseball." The text was short because it was sent from the patient's iPhone (as the signature on the email attested) at 4:30 a.m. in the morning: "My testicles are the size of a baseball. Should I increase the diuretics? Thank you." In college, when email was just starting to become popular,

I used to obsess over the subject headings I put on my emails, desperate to be clever. Once, I emailed a woman I was pursuing with the subject "Cedric Ceballos," a relatively obscure NBA player whose only claim to fame was winning the slam dunk contest with a blindfolded dunk. We traded dozens of emails, each with the subject "re: Cedric Ceballos," but never directly discussed (over email, or in person on our single date) why I'd chosen that subject. Likewise, I've never told this patient how much I appreciated his subject heading, but I think about it every time I see him. I also use his email (with all of the identifiers blacked out) in a slide at the beginning of my lecture on edema management, because it never fails to get a good laugh from the audience.

Technology has clearly altered doctor-patient dynamics. It's not just patients now having access to the internet's unlimited trove of "medical information," much of which has not been vetted by reliable experts. And it's not just patients texting with their doctors, sending them friend requests on Facebook, retweeting them on Twitter, and emailing them at all hours of the day. The new generation of doctors is a generation of technically savvy texters and emailers and tweeters, and their version of doctoring is highly integrated with technology in a language that their predecessors, like my father, can't fully understand.

In a story from NPR on the increased use of technology by the newest generation of doctors (NPR called them "millennial doctors"), Dr. Rick Snyder, a Texas cardiologist "from the baby boom generation" discussed his worries that young doctors would not forge the same relationships with their patients as his peers did. He compared young doctors today to young soldiers in Vietnam who became over-reliant on technology at the cost of their dogfighting skills. "We as physicians, that's our dogfighting skills: talking to a patient, interacting with a patient," Snyder said. The same story quoted a recent medical school graduate on how technology had made her last four years of study much easier than expected: "I would wake up at 10 a.m., work out for an hour or so, get some lunch and then video stream for 6 hours and then go to happy hour. It actually was not that bad."[1]

A group of physicians from the Washington, DC, VA Medical Center set out to describe "the characteristics of self-identified physicians on Twitter and how they use Twitter, with a specific focus on professionalism." In the *Journal of the American Medical Association*, they reported that 3 percent of physician tweets were "unprofessional," with the offenses ranging from potential patient-privacy violations to sexually explicit material and discriminatory statements.[2] Kevin O'Reilly, writing in the American Medical Association's newsletter, found that "physicians who write anonymously online say it affords them the opportunity to vent their frustrations with patients, colleagues, administrators and health plans with less fear of crossing legal and ethical lines."[3]

"Suburban Physician," the anonymous physician behind the Twitter feed @BurbDoc, has become a cult hero for a growing

(>7,000 followers) bunch of online physicians who (based on virtually all of his tweets being liked or retweeted) agree with him when he tweets, "Remember, folks, it's not that I don't care, it's just that I dislike certain patients." Or when he tweets, "Local specialist is very LOUD about his Christian faith. Called him up abt a poss charity case, simple fix, on an uninsured pt. Said no thx." Or when he tweets, "Now when I get past med records from prior docs, it's a tome bigger than Moby Dick's dick. Seriously. NYC's Yellow Pages is smaller." If my father, who is probably going to have to surrender to retirement because the onslaught of electronic medical records has completely undermined his efficiency as a physician, ever learned how to use Twitter, he could like or retweet, "Clicking stupid fucking boxes isn't about best care. It's about datamining our charts so some higher up fuckwad can demand more salary."

I never signed up for Facebook because I didn't want to have to deal with the awkwardness of denying a patient's friend request. I use Facebook to keep track of old friends, but I do so via Xenia's account. I use Twitter, but the subjects of my tweets are limited to sports, music, literature, film— essentially, any topic other than medicine. About half of the accounts that follow mine, though, are doctors, nurses, patients, or medical societies, because I've identified myself as a physician in my Twitter bio. I have a recurring joke on Twitter (it's funny to me, at least) in which I take quotes from authors, poets, or songwriters and downgrade them via attachment to my favorite sports teams. For example, David Berman's line, "Repair is the dream of the broken thing," is recast as in-depth analysis of the Mets' futile attempt to execute a squeeze bunt. I tweeted out an Arthur Miller quote—"If I see an ending, I can work backward"—labeling it Derek Fisher's explanation of his fourth-quarter coaching strategy for the bumbling Knicks. Someone named @TransplantHQ modified that tweet by affixing the hashtag "#transplant." I read his Twitter biography: "Had a kidney transplant, went to medical school, and trying to figure out how it all fits together." His re-purposing of my tweet suggests he has figured something out.

In an email with the subject, "The state of my body and mind," my patient asked me to stop a medication I'd prescribed at her last visit. "The side effects, which range from debilitating to annoying, are too much for me," she wrote. "In fact, I am sending this by email rather than talking to you directly because one of the debilitating side effects is that I am always depressed and, as a result, I am too emotional right now to talk to you." She then proceeded to list all of her side effects—cramping, diarrhea, depression, loss of appetite, hair loss from the top of her head, hair growth on her face, itchy nose, throat congestion, skin rash, peeling nails, sore and bleeding gums, bad taste in the mouth, sour breath, and "a very emotional state. When I did go to the theater, at the end of the play, I was sobbing. Nobody else was crying. Driving in my car, an old Roy Orbison song that had no particular meaning to me made me cry." This last part didn't seem so bad to me, because the Roy Orbison song I reflexively thought of was "Crying," which has always stirred up something sad inside me, too. Later, when I reread the email just before calling her, it occurred to me that the Roy Orbison song may have been "Pretty Woman," and the despair my patient was trying to convey in that email became so much more apparent.

The same patient, in an earlier email with the subject "Lavender Monster Pills," wrote: "You promised me no horse pills, but these are the biggest pills I have ever seen—over 3/4 of an inch! Before I try swallowing these tomorrow, is this my only size option? I sometimes choke on Citracal Petites which are even smaller than these monsters. . . . BTW, they are lavender—is that supposed to make them more palatable?" In both instances, I can't say for sure that she would have been so open with me, so willing to appear vulnerable and ask for help, without the safe distance that email provides. Our face-to-face encounters in the clinic had never been particularly intimate or emotional. I'd seen her laugh, but I'd never seen her cry.

I stopped the medicine. A few months later, when she was in my office, smiling and telling me how great she felt, I asked, "So no more crying from Roy Orbison songs?" She did not remember the email, so I reminded her about the exchange. "I think I've just blocked out that entire episode," she offered as an explanation. She emailed me that night, though: "I remembered on the way home. The Roy Orbison song was 'Running Scared,' a song that actually has a happy ending." I didn't know the song, so I immediately pulled up

YouTube to listen, and the song's opening lines almost made *me* cry: "Just running scared, each place we go, so afraid, that he might show." But I listened to the end, and she was right. The song does have a happy ending.

"I type all my notes," I tell my new patients, my fingers perched on the keyboard. "So that means sometimes I have to look at my screen, but I'm always listening to you." As a medical student, I was told to maintain eye contact with patients at all times. Look between their eyebrows, I was advised, if looking directly into their eyes was too difficult. The patients won't be able to tell the difference. Patients often look down or to the side when they tell their stories, but when they do take the opportunity to look at their doctors, their doctors better be looking right back at them. Now, as a constantly typing clinician, my head is on a swivel, back and forth between the computer screen and the patients' eyes (or the space between their eyebrows).

The large, multispecialty group that bought my father's practice and now employs him provided a scribe for his transition to their electronic medical record. None of his partners, who are in their forties and fifties, are using this service, but my father seems to like having the help. "I still have to check over what she types," my father says. "It's still slower than just writing the notes myself by hand, but at least it gets me away from the computer while I'm seeing patients." Translation: He can still look his patients in the eyes.

7 WHAT ARE THEIR NAMES?

By his two-month appointment, Mateo was a different baby. "Pretty much as soon as I cut out dairy," Xenia dutifully reported to Dr. Owens, our pediatrician, "he stopped being so fussy. And now, he's smiling and cooing, and we even heard him laugh yesterday for the first time." Dr. Owens smiled and nodded approval at his progress. "The only thing, though," Xenia added, "is that he still has really mucousy poops, and we started checking his stools with Hemoccult cards, and there's always blood in them."

Dr. Owens smiled again. She talked to us while examining Mateo. She was looking at him, speaking into his face with a baby-talk voice, but addressing us. Moving his little legs with a bicycle kick, she said, "So it sounds like he's made some big improvements but is not all the way there." She recommended Xenia stay off dairy and also cut out soy from her diet. She also advised us to give Mateo a probiotic powder every evening, dissolved in a bottle of expressed breast milk.

I vowed to be home from work every day before 6:00 p.m. so I could give him that bottle.

Juno asked if she could take the probiotic, too, when she saw me dumping the lactobacillus granules into Mateo's bottle. The wrapper was bright yellow with green writing, easily mistaken for a treat and not a treatment.

"I want one," she said.

"This is *medicina*," I said, "and it's just for babies."

"But I want *medicina*," she said.

She marched out of the kitchen, into her room, and started to cry. We'd been working with her on this method of coping ever since Mateo was born. "It's okay to be upset, and it's okay to cry," we'd told her, reciting lines we'd read in a parenting book. "You can go to your room, have a good cry, and when you're ready for Mommy or Daddy to come get you, just call for us." I listened to her crying as I rolled Mateo's bottle in my hand to stir the probiotic powder.

"Daddy," Juno yelled from her room, "I'm ready for you!"

The next day, on the way home from work, I stopped at the pharmacy to buy her chewable probiotic tablets, each individually wrapped in a yellow packet with green lettering.

I was on-call and told Juno, just as she was going down for her midday nap, that I needed to go into the hospital to see some sick patients. "What are their names?" she asked.

Her question made me laugh, and when I repeated it to Xenia, she laughed too. It's the kind of question only a patient would ask and only a doctor would have problems answering. Sure, we know our patients' names and their medical histories, their diagnoses and their medications. In the best cases, we also know their families—their anxious spouses, doting parents, adorable kids, recently deceased pets—and might even speak, at the beginning and end of appointments, in a friendly, informal manner more befitting a backyard barbecue than a doctor's office. In truth, though, we only know what the patients are willing to share with us.

Sometimes we're lucky enough to have something resembling intimacy with our patients, when our communication breaks free from all the formalities of doctor-patient speak. My recently transplanted patient asked me if he could attend his niece's Christmas pageant. "Sure," I said. "You can pretty much do whatever you like at this point, as long as you use common sense about washing your hands and avoid close contact with people who are obviously sick." He registered the advice and sat quietly. "Do you want to go?" I asked. "Not really," he said. "Then you can say I told you not to go," I offered.

Sometimes I do feel as if I'm privy to a patient's private world. I was excited to call a patient to review her lab results, which were good. I knew she'd be happy to hear that her kidney function had improved significantly over the last three months. I got the answering machine. It was her husband's voice. At her first appointment, about four years earlier, she'd mentioned her husband had died within the past year. She was on antidepressants at that time to help her grieving process, medications she'd subsequently stopped.

She now had a new boyfriend, the man she'd jokingly called her chauffer at the last visit. I waited for her dead husband to finish the answering machine greeting and left a message.

Sometimes I have to force the intimacy, or in the very least let the patient know that it's okay for us to communicate with real words. A patient did not believe me when I said it had been three years since his last appointment, so I swiveled the computer monitor to show him the clinic's electronic schedule as proof. "That's too long for someone with kidney disease," I said. Fortunately, his health had, if anything, improved during that time, so there were no obvious consequences to all those missed appointments. "But I probably would have been able to get you on less medication if we'd seen each other during those three years. You're taking more pills now than you need." He absorbed my rebuke and promised he would get labs every four months and see me every six months. As he was leaving the exam room, I said, "Look, if it makes you feel any better, my dentist gave me the same lecture at my last appointment because I hadn't seen her in three years." The patient smiled. I added, "But my teeth aren't as important as your kidneys." He smiled wider.

Just as often, though, I'm confronted with how little I know about my patients. In most instances, doctors and patients are just playing roles for each other. I do this all the time, from both ends of the exam table. I use the lower register of my voice and try to sound like Don Draper from *Mad Men* when it's important that my patients buy into everything I say. "This medicine will work, but only if you take it exactly as it's prescribed," I might say in my Don Draper voice, even though both parts of that sentence are partially inaccurate (i.e., the efficacy rate is only about 75 percent, and a missed pill here and there won't affect therapeutic drug levels). And when I visit the dentist, I flat out lie about how often I floss. I play these roles because I believe that my patients want a confident, TV-like doctor and my dentist wants a patient who follows her instructions. Does all this role-playing actually bring doctors and patients closer together or, unintentionally, further drive a wedge between us?

"He didn't want to say anything at the last visit," my patient's wife said on the phone. "But on the ride home he was crying. You know, we've accepted that he's going into kidney failure, that he's going to need a transplant, but it's still hard on him," she continued. "He can't sleep. He's a nervous wreck. He just doesn't want you to know that."

I told her his reaction was perfectly normal. I told her it would be abnormal if he'd reacted any other way to such bad news. I employed my Don Draper voice.

"Do you think he should take Xanax?" she asked.

"No," I answered, breaking back into my regular voice, "but I only see him every few weeks, and you see him every day. Do you think he should take Xanax? If yes, I'll prescribe it."

Mateo's aunts and uncles marveled at how "good" a baby he was. They said they'd never heard him cry, and these claims, while somewhat exaggerated, were not too far from the truth.

He hardly ever cried now, whereas in his first month, before Xenia cut dairy out of her diet, he cried all the time. He writhed while being fed and screamed any time he was out of a tight swaddle. The only thing that seemed to calm him down was an almost violent form of burping that Xenia, my mother-in-law, and I did around the clock. He was so miserable that I avoided being around him, using the "it's important for Juno and me to have some one-on-one time" excuse as I snuck away with her to a playground or the public library or the bagel store.

Within days of Xenia's elimination of dairy from her diet, Mateo transformed into an angel baby. He smiled and laughed at two months, far ahead of the baby books' schedule for such milestones. His eyes radiated a kindness and eagerness to be happy I'd never seen in Juno's eyes (nor in mine or Xenia's eyes, either). And, as others pointed out, he essentially stopped crying. I considered this non-crying just another one of his saintly traits.

"Our house is so loud already," I said, "and he doesn't want to add to all the noise pollution."

Xenia theorized, "He had so much real pain as a newborn that he learned to only associate crying with pain. He doesn't cry when he's hungry or has poop like other babies, only when he's in pain."

Mateo was the kind of patient doctors appreciate: the patient who never cries wolf.

The patients I most appreciate tend to be young. They have positive outlooks. They deal with their illnesses much better than I would if I were in their shoes. I look forward to their visits in a way that I don't with other patients. I ease up with them and feel more like myself in the way I talk. I never use the Don Draper voice.

The digital thermometer in my office has two probes, red and blue. As far as I know, the probes are interchangeable. If one of my favorite patients asks about the difference between the probes, I always make the same joke. If I just took a temperature with the red probe, I casually say that the red probe is for taking rectal temperatures and the blue probe is for taking oral temperatures. I wouldn't try that joke on just any patient.

However, the distance between doctor and patient never completely goes away, even in the best circumstance. We—and by we, I mean both doctors and patients—can probably only hope for this distance to merely shrink. I said to one of my favorite patients, a man in his mid-twenties who'd lost his kidneys due to lupus and was now on dialysis, waiting for a kidney transplant, "You have such a great attitude. You're always so optimistic. I admire you so much. It's got to be hard to keep that spirit up." He answered, "No, I break down, I break down a lot, but in my home, with my family. I don't need to do that in a doctor's office." I've thought about this exchange at all of his subsequent appointments, even visits in which we've discussed how well he's doing since his kidney transplant.

In medical school, a senior attending told my class, "If you've done your job right, then the patient should trust you enough to ask what to do in difficult situations. Sometimes they phrase it differently. What would you recommend for your wife or your son or some other family member? But it's essentially the same question of, 'What should I do?' If your patients ask you that, then you've done your job. And if you answer them directly, then you're failing them. Our job is to build up trust and educate patients in these critical moments. We share our expertise. We empower them." But we still must keep our distance.

Saying goodbye to Juno in the morning, I told her I wouldn't be home until after she fell asleep. "*Nos vemos en la mañana*," I said. She asked me why. I lied and told her I had to work late; in truth, I was going straight from work to a Mets game.

"But why do you have to work late?" she asked. And then she offered me a better answer than I would have ever come up with on my own: "There's lots of *enfermos* in the hospital?"

"*Sí*," I said.

8 HIGHLY ATTENTIVE MEDICINE

My fellow, who is having difficulty finding a nephrology job, asked me whether she should take a position in a general internal medicine practice. "In the beginning," she said, "I'd be mostly primary care, but the goal would be that the other docs referred their nephrology cases to me, so that in three or four years I'd have a practice that was just about a third primary care and two-thirds nephrology." She asked for my honest opinion.

"Honestly," I joked, "nothing gives me more pleasure than telling a patient, 'I'm here to focus on your kidneys. The rest is for your primary care physician.'" We laughed, but I do say that line at least once or twice a week.

Concierge medicine is an agreement between a patient and a primary care physician in which the patient pays an annual fee, and, in exchange, the physician provides enhanced care, including a commitment to limit patient loads to ensure adequate time and availability for each patient. The availability is an important feature: the doctor can be reached, in some agreements, 24 hours a day, 7 days a week, 365 days a year. Concierge medicine has also been called retainer medicine, membership medicine, VIP medicine, cash-only practice, and direct care.

The origins of concierge medicine are often traced to MD² International, which was launched in 1996 by Howard Maron. Dr. Maron, though, does not like the terminology, explaining, "I know what a concierge is, but to describe what I do as simply opening doors and directing people. . . . I prefer highly attentive medicine."[1] When I'm staying in a hotel, I never take the time to learn the concierge's name. I refer to him or her simply as "the concierge," as in "let's ask the concierge to make us a dinner reservation." I've never heard patients call their doctors "concierge doctors"—it's a term that appears in newspaper and magazine articles, and it's a label doctors use derisively to refer to certain doctors.

I write Propecia prescriptions for my best friend from college, even though he has fuller hair than I do. I also call in a five-day course of antibiotics every time he has a cold, although this would not be my routine practice if a patient complained of similar, viral-like symptoms. My father writes Ambien prescriptions for my mother; together, they take about two years to go through a bottle of 30 pills. I prescribe Valtrex for Xenia so she can always have them on hand just in case she feels a cold sore coming on. Most doctors are concierge physicians for their family and friends.

Because I work at a top-ten university hospital in a top-five ranked nephrology division (both according to *US News & World Report*), and because I have a strong "internet resume," I often see referrals from concierge physicians. "Only the best for my patients," I imagine these concierge physicians saying. Some of these referrals never needed to see a kidney specialist, the work easily handled by a competent primary care physician. Some of the referrals turn out to be gross mismanagement. The majority, though, are appropriate referrals that have been appropriately managed. I'd make the same tally regarding my referrals from non-concierge physicians. The only tangible differences are that the patients referred by concierge practices are wealthier, appear more satisfied with their primary care doctors, and expect a more intimate relationship that I cannot offer. They are used to texting and emailing their concierge physicians at any time of day, and they often express amazement that I would still require them to call my office, speak to a secretary, and wait for a call back from me.

A recent trend is a more affordable version of concierge medicine: the JCPenney version of concierge medicine. The *Wall Street Journal* profiled "a new and growing generation of concierge doctors who, in this era of health reform, see more opportunity in the middle class than they do in the jet set." The article described a chain of 16 primary care clinics in five states that charged $59 a month for membership with an additional $10 charge per visit, with no billing of insurance at any point. The trend has "bifurcated the retainer medicine industry: On one end, patients pay thousands of dollars a month for lavish celebrity-type treatment at traditional concierge practices. On the other, pared-down clinics charge roughly $50 to $100 a month for basic primary care medicine, more accessible doctors, and yes, money savings for those looking to reduce their health spending."[2] Lower-end concierge practices charge patients directly for treatment, posting menu-style prices for services and requiring payment up front.

Time magazine, in an article describing the newer model of affordable, budget-friendly concierge medicine, asked, "Would ordinary people pay the equivalent of a monthly cable bill for the satisfaction of having a doctor who knew their histories and cheerfully answered their questions?" The answer, according to *Time*, was a resounding yes, exemplified by the success of Qliance Health, an affordable concierge company in Seattle that serves over 35,000 patients, about half of whom are on Medicaid.[3] The Walmart version of concierge medicine.

Patients will pay for concierge medicine because they know, or believe they know, what they are buying. The concierge physician aligns with their vision of a doctor whose sole purpose is to serve his or her patients. I often have difficulty understanding exactly what non-physicians do for a living. I hear their job titles, listen to their job descriptions, but still wonder what exactly they're doing from 8:00 a.m. to 5:00 p.m. each day. In contrast, when I tell someone I'm a doctor, I know they immediately form a picture of how my day is spent, moving from one patient to the next. It's the only version of a doctor most people know, the one they've seen from the perspective of a patient sitting on an exam table. Yet, that's not really how my day is spent—or, more specifically, that's only how three of the ten half-days of my work week are spent. I've charted out my career to avoid having the type of day where I move from one patient to the next, the way community doctors like my father do.

In elementary school, my friends and I repeatedly asked my father questions about sex. We were probably eight or nine when we did this. We knew how he'd respond. He always gave us the same answer: a straightforward, clinical rendition of intercourse. He talked of penises and vaginas, fallopian tubes and ovaries, seminal vesicles and sperm. We listened to him with the straightest of faces and waited for him to leave before cracking up. I wonder how I'll answer questions about sex from Juno and Mateo. Will I feel an obligation to biology, as I'm sure my father did, and relay an honest, scientific answer? I can't picture myself or my father talking about storks or baby fairies or daddies magically placing babies inside mommies' bellies. My father told us about placentas and umbilical cords. I'll probably do the same.

My friends and I laughed at my father's words—"the man inserts his penis into the woman's vagina"—but we never laughed at him. When we recited back his descriptions of sex, we never imitated his stutter. We respected him and his knowledge too much for that kind of ridicule. I should mention that my father was my friends' pediatrician. He took care of many of my brothers' friends, too. All of our neighbors. Most of our classmates. Our number was listed in the phone book, and sometimes he'd get called on nights when he wasn't technically on call. He'd answer parents' questions and then politely remind them of the on-call doctor, whom they should contact if anything else came up that night. He was a concierge physician before the term existed. Today's patients like the idea of concierge doctors because these doctors remind them of the legendary doctors of their childhood, even if these were just doctors from television shows or books or, in the special cases like my father, real life doctors who loved caring for patients so much that they were happy to continue doctoring whenever someone needed their help. A collective nostalgia for these doctors-who-never-stop-being-doctors helped the idea of a concierge physician take hold in popular consciousness.

At weekend soccer games, if an injury occurred on the field, all the parents on the sideline turned to my father. If he stayed in place and let the coach take care of the injured player, the other parents relaxed. But if he crossed the sideline and entered the field of play, especially if he jogged over to the fallen child, the other parents held their breaths. The most powerful parent on the sideline was the coach, because he determined who played and who didn't. But the second most powerful parent on the sideline was my father, the doctor.

9 IT'S COMPLICATED

I went to medical school with Holly. We were friendly but not necessarily friends. She's now a pulmonologist in my hospital. We say hello to each other when we pass in the hallway or sometimes just wave. The other day we were walking in the same direction. I asked her, "How's it going?"

She replied, "Not too great. I just caused a pneumothorax and have to tell this guy he'll need a chest tube."

"I'm sorry," I said.

"This sucks," she said.

"I feel like complications are just a reflection of volume," I said. "Jim Cooper has the most biopsy complications in our division because he does about ten times more biopsies than any of the rest of us."

By invoking Jim Cooper's name, I was consoling Holly. Jim is one of the most respected nephrologists in our hospital, and he and Holly share a number of patients (lung transplant patients who subsequently get kidney failure). We could find solace, I thought, in his complication rate. Regardless, this was probably the most unguarded conversation we'd ever had.

All divisions conduct a monthly, or quarterly, or biannual "M&M" conference: morbidity and mortality. Cases are chosen for discussion if they involved a poor outcome, including death, and if this poor outcome may have been avoidable. The case is usually presented by the physician who cared for the patient, under whose watch the bad outcome occurred, and the trial is by a jury of his or her peers. The conference is considered the ultimate example of constructive criticism. Together, as a group, the division decides whether an outcome, including death, should or should not have occurred. In cases where the outcome did not have to occur, the division creates an action plan to prevent similar events in the future.

My colleague presented a post-biopsy bleed at our last M&M conference. The patient ultimately died during the hospitalization, and the biopsy complication was arguably the main contributor to that death. My colleague identified some of the features in the patient's history that made the biopsy higher risk than the average procedure, including the patient's age, recent use of a blood thinner, and underlying cirrhosis. He then opened the discussion up to questions and comments. The first question came from one of the most senior physicians in our division: "Did you even need to do the biopsy?" There was some awkward laughter, but the questioner persisted. "What exactly did you expect to find on a biopsy in this patient that would have changed management? To me, the thing to learn about this case isn't how to predict biopsy complications as much as when a biopsy is unnecessary, because I don't think this biopsy should have been done in the first place."

When Xenia attends on the hospital teaching service, she tells her residents to consider MRB, maximum resident benefit, versus MPB, maximum patient benefit, before doing a procedure. "Ask yourselves, 'Am I doing this procedure for MRB or for the patient? If I have a complication during this procedure, would it have been worth it for the patient?' Because if you do have a complication, you want to feel justified in having done the procedure." She learned the MRB and MPB acronyms when she was an intern, passed on by a wise upper-level resident. I think back to my own time in the ICU as an intern. My upper-level resident was a bit of a "cowboy," which is resident-speak for someone who likes to do procedures. "You're going to put a central line in every admission we get," he said on my first day, "and by the end of the month you'll be the best one in your class at doing lines." I nodded. He continued, "You can basically justify putting in a central line in any patient who needs ICU level care."

Doctors can talk themselves into or out of pretty much anything.

A small scar sits just beneath Xenia's right armpit: a raised, white X that marks where surgeons emergently placed a chest tube to drain blood from her lungs. This happened a few years before we met. She'd been diagnosed with a blood clot in her right arm and had been given a thrombolytic, an intravenous clot-busting agent that, if successful, yields rapid resolution of the blood clot. The medicine, however, also imparts an increased risk for bleeding. When she talks about the complication, whether it's in bed as I run my index finger over that X or in a didactic exercise about medical errors with her residents, she never blames the thoracic surgeon who administered the drug. "It was a questionable call to give lytics," she concedes, "but he was just trying to be as aggressive as possible with an otherwise healthy young patient. And I knew the risk of bleeding."

She does, however, blame her nurse. "She thought I was making it up, that I was drug seeking, and I kept telling her my chest was burning." When Xenia got out of bed to use the bathroom, her heart rate skyrocketed, her blood pressure dropped, and she nearly passed out. The on-call doctor was paged and, without examining her, recommended she be placed back in bed in Trendelenburg position, with the feet about 30° higher than the head. If Xenia had sued (she didn't), this on-call doctor (she never learned his name) would be the defendant.

The next morning, when her thoracic surgeon returned to see her, her heart rate was up into the 150s and her blood pressure was down into the sixties. The morning labs showed she'd lost about five units of blood overnight, and an X-ray confirmed the blood was in her lungs. Soon, with just a small amount of local anesthesia, a large tube was inserted into her lung cavity to drain the blood. She obviously survived, got better, and has just a dime-sized scar on her chest as a souvenir. "The complication couldn't have been prevented," she says, "but it wouldn't have been so severe and so dangerous if that nurse had just listened to me and if that on-call doctor had just examined me. And the sad thing is, I doubt anyone ever told either of them what happened. They probably have no idea about how they almost let me die."

A professor in medical school, when teaching the differential diagnosis, urged us to start with an easy acronym: F.T.D. (like the florist). First Think Drugs. Side effects. Complications of therapy. "Remember that every medication a doctor prescribes a patient is, at its essence, a non-natural substance, a potential poison," the professor warned us. Always start from the notion that a patient's illness could be due to the unintended consequences of his or her doctor trying to help.

We learn more from our mistakes and failures than from any of our successes. This is probably true in every aspect of life but is one of the core tenets of medicine. This is what I tell my students, residents, and fellows when they've committed an error. "We learn from our mistakes and failures" would be an accurate slogan for any academic medical center, even though the subtext of this maxim is that we learn at the expense of our patients' health and, in some instances, their lives.

For his fifteenth birthday, I took my nephew to see his favorite comedian, Demetri Martin, who specializes in short, witty jokes that micro-inspect our world. Sample joke: "There's a fine line between having a pet and holding another species hostage." One of the loudest laughs of the night came when Martin expressed disbelief that people still died of surgical complications. "These are not new surgeries," he said, "so I'd expect that by this point they shouldn't be complicated." Laughter. "I'm sorry, but your husband died on the operating table. The surgery was complicated." Laughter. "Complicated? Yes, complicated. The doctor ate something bad for lunch, the nurse was in a grumpy mood, there was a creepy medical student who was observing and he gave everyone the jitters, so, yes, it was complicated."

The word "complication" does a disservice to doctors because it implies that the right mind or situation could have solved the problem. I can't think of a better alternative to *complication*, though. The most accurate term would incorporate the concept of luck—specifically, bad luck. A term that captures how much of a role fortune plays would make complications more understandable for both the patient and the doctor.

On the other hand, the role of luck, good or bad, is one of the secrets of medicine, shared by both patients (who want to believe that their doctors are immune to the whims of fortune) and doctors (who want to believe the exact same thing). Yet, in friendly settings, doctors will often trade stories with each other that betray our superstitions. I now always wear brown shoes when I do a kidney biopsy because my two worst bleeds occurred on days when I wore black shoes. My fellows know this, but my patients don't.

I've been fortunate to have had only two major complications at this point in my career. Both were post-biopsy bleeds requiring inpatient hospitalizations and continuous bladder irrigation to flush out clots that the biopsy had caused. Neither required further intervention beyond the bladder irrigation, which was done through a penile catheter. Both patients were young men whom I'd seen numerous times in clinic; we had a relationship and a degree of trust prior to the complication that allowed me to say "I'm sorry" with the utmost sincerity and, more importantly, allowed them to believe my apology. I saw them every day they were in the hospital, as a social visit rather than as a medical visit, and I called them the day after their discharges as a form of closure. As far as major complications go, these experiences were unusually benign. I felt guilty while the patients were in the hospital, but as soon as I hung up the phone after their post-discharge phone calls, I was ready to move on to other patients and other issues.

My father doesn't have a single blemish on his record, as far as I know. In a career that spans five decades, he's never once been named in a malpractice suit, a feat even more impressive given that he's devoted about a third of his time to the pediatric emergency room for the last twenty-five years.

About ten years ago, when he was struggling with a prolonged depression, my father beat himself up over missing a diagnosis. He said the depression was affecting the way he thought and, in turn, was affecting the way he doctored.

When I asked him for more details about the case, though, it turned out he didn't miss the diagnosis. It just took him longer than he expected of himself to make the diagnosis. He admitted most pediatricians would have never made the diagnosis even with unlimited time. And the child's parents sent my father a huge fruit basket that Christmas with a note thanking him for saving their child's life.

10 AND IT WILL LAST FOREVER

An elderly patient of mine who has done quite well in his life relayed one of his core philosophies: "You want to have an old lawyer but a young doctor." He'd rather have an energetic doctor than an experienced one.

What does it mean that I've devoted myself to a career because I wanted to be like my father, and yet the profession is now pushing doctors like him out to make space for doctors like me? I don't know the answer to that question. I know I've accepted and even, at times, welcomed his being pushed out, because his practice is no longer the kind of medicine he wants to do. He can't keep up with the language of modern medicine, and, ironically, this has nothing to do with the stutter that's plagued him his entire life.

In sports, we praise the athletes who retire when they're still at or close to their peak powers, and we lament the superstars who've hung around too long. They tarnish their reputations and alienate the fans with their poor performances until someone else (i.e., a team owner refusing to offer another contract) decides it's time for them to retire. My father is the Willie Mays of pediatrics (a good sentence for his obituary), and his final years of taking care of children could be as disastrous as the end of Mays's career. I deride the older doctors that I work with, the ones who've hung around too long, yet I don't want younger pediatricians (or, even worse, new patients) to do this to my father. But could I blame these fresh-faced doctors for doing so, when the only version of Dr. Bomback they know is an anxious, white-haired doctor who keeps asking them for help with the electronic medical record?

When my father and his partners sold their practice to a large multispecialty group, the terms of the sale included shutting down their current office location and moving to a medical complex owned by their new employer. "It was hard," my father said about packing up his old office. "I'd been there almost 30 years." I remember when he brought my mother, my brothers, and me to that office. It was still unfurnished, but the space was bright and clean and brand new, a distinct change from the office space he and his two other partners had been using. He was so excited. We were excited for him. Those two other partners retired over twenty years ago, and the practice has grown to six pediatricians: six pediatricians who now work for someone else, in someone else's office space. "Did you cry?" I asked my father. I meant the question as a joke, but he answered in complete sincerity, "A little."

I took the morning off to accompany Xenia to Mateo's four-month-old check-up visit. Xenia had been off dairy and soy for three months, but Mateo was still showing signs of an allergic colitis. His stools were normal in color, but they often contained flecks of blood. Even when we couldn't see blood in his diaper, we always got a strongly positive result when we tested for blood with fecal Hemoccult cards.

Our pediatrician is one of my father's partners. Like the other partners in the practice, she trained under my father during residency. This was my first visit to their new office, which took up a third of a floor in a brand-new, ten story medical complex. I was already feeling down about how sterile and corporate the new office felt when I overheard the receptionist talking on the phone to a parent of a sick child. "I'm sorry," the receptionist said, "but the only doctor with an available slot today is Dr. Bomback, so if you want to do a walk-in visit, it will have to be with Dr. Bomback." After a pause, the receptionist said, "Yes, of course, Dr. Bomback works very closely with Dr. Owens." Another pause, and then, "Okay, so I'll put you in for Dr. Bomback at 3:15 today."

My father used to be the celebrity of the practice, the doctor for whom families were willing to wait weeks to months for a new appointment, the doctor whose schedule was so jam-packed that he often needed to give his overflow to his junior partners, like Dr. Owens, our pediatrician. I still ran everything Dr. Owens said by my father after our appointment. I wanted to make sure he approved of her recommendations, although I knew it was unnecessary. I knew it might have been more for my father's sake and mine than for Mateo's.

I wonder what my father does in between patients now that his patient panel isn't full. On my clinic days, on the rare occasions that I have downtime between patients, I check email, read websites like Vulture and Pitchfork, and scroll through Twitter. It's hard for me to imagine my father wasting time with any of these internet-oriented activities, particularly in the presence of the scribe who's been hired to follow him around and whose Eastern European name he can't pronounce (he calls her "T," as do all of his nurses).

It's possible that when he laments how he's not filling his schedule the way he used to, when his panel was crammed with patients and last-minute add-ons who refused to see anyone other than Dr. Bomback, he's undercutting his own efforts. He still might be zipping from one patient to the next. That's the only way I can picture him in his office, bouncing in and out of exam rooms, never taking a break. I'd bet that's the only way he can picture himself working, too.

My mentor from fellowship, who is about three years younger than my father, just retired. Reading between the lines, it appears that he was essentially forced into retirement by his division chief. He didn't say the word "ageism," but the schedule he'd been given had more away rotations and more months on service than in any previous year. The implied message from the division chief: if you don't like this schedule, it will be easy to find a younger doctor with a lower salary to do the same work. With the sale of his practice, my father is now technically an employee. At some point his bosses might question why they shouldn't replace him with someone younger who can see more patients and who doesn't need to be followed around by a scribe.

I was on the subway, heading toward the hospital on a Sunday morning and feeling sorry for myself that I had to work on a weekend. I scanned the advertisements hanging above the seats and stopped at one of the MTA's sponsored placards from their Poetry in Motion series. I read "Heaven," by Patrick Phillips, the last line of which scans: "It will be the past. And it will last forever."[1] As an academic physician, I only have to work five weekends a year—my "grumpy weekends," to steal from Xenia. My dad works about twice that number of weekends. He used to work every third weekend when my brothers and I were young, when he only had two partners. He never seemed grumpy when he came home late on a Saturday afternoon, telling my mother how many sick kids he'd seen that day. The numbers meant nothing to me then—what was twenty-five sick kids, forty sick kids, fifty sick kids?—but now I realize just how difficult those weekend mornings would have been for a doctor who didn't love his work. His partners from that time retired more than two decades ago. My dad still plugs away, working more weekends than his son. Heaven is the past, and, if my dad could somehow will it to be true, the past would last forever.

I want my father to retire because medicine is drifting further and further away from the kind of doctoring he loves. His idea of what a doctor does is not that different from Juno's. Both envision a physician walking into a room where a sick patient awaits a doctor's magic. Both envision that physician listening, then touching, then healing. I'd like to think that Juno's romantic version comes from being the daughter of two doctors, the niece of another doctor, the granddaughter of yet another doctor. But her version might just as well be based on the Disney cartoon *Doc McStuffins*, whose Spanish-translated episodes she watches on an iPad.

My father's version also aligns closely with the way doctors are depicted on screen, but his version comes directly from his own experiences, his own exalted past. Both my daughter and my father are set up for disillusionment. My father's has already begun, I know, when he confesses that he doesn't look forward to going to work as much as he used to.

My sister-in-law takes her kids to see Dr. Flannagan, another one of my father's junior partners. She and Dr. Flannagan have more intimate conversations than Xenia and I have with Dr. Owens. She and Dr. Flannagan talk about my father. "She told me that she can tell your father's depressed again," my sister-in-law relayed. "All the partners know it, and they all know it's tied into not feeling needed as much in the office. She said that the last time your father was depressed, which was about ten years ago, right after he turned sixty, they were worried he wouldn't snap out of it. But then there was a case in the ER, and none of the pediatricians could figure it out, until your dad went in to see the boy, looked in his ears, and made the diagnosis in an instant. And apparently it was like, snap, all of a sudden he wasn't depressed anymore. At least at work."

I said, "I just don't see that kind of moment happening for him again."

"Neither does Emma," my sister-in-law said. She's on a first name basis with Dr. Flannagan.

Emma's probably right. I didn't need confirmation but got it anyway from a new patient whose chart included a detailed summary of his medical records, printed out on his own medical stationary.

"What kind of doctor are you?" I asked.

"A pediatrician," he said.

"Oh, do you know my father?" I asked.

"That's why I made an appointment with you," he said.

The patient was seven years younger than my father and had cut down his practice to only two days a week. I told him my father was still working full-time with no immediate plans to retire. He knew that, and he also knew that my father and his partners had sold the practice.

"It's a great move for everyone except your dad," the patient said.

I let the comment hang in the air for a moment.

"Okay, well, let's figure out your kidneys," I said.

My mentor has a second home in rural Virginia, which he calls "the farm" because of its tremendous garden. "I'd be on the farm for a week, and I'd feel like that was my real self," he said. "And then I'd come back to work, and I felt like an imposter for a week or two, like I was putting on an act for the patients. And they bought it. And after a week or two of feeling like that, eventually I'd buy my own act, and then I'd feel like a doctor again." He told me this at his retirement party when I commented on how happy he looked.

My father would never relate to that story or to those feelings. He's always felt most like himself with a white coat on and a stethoscope clasped around his neck. He's always smiling when he's in his office, bouncing from patient to patient. He's always had only one hobby: medicine. When someone asks him when he'll retire, his response is to ask back, "What would I do if I retire?"

I ask my older physician patients when they retired or, if they're still practicing, when they are going to retire. I ask friends whose parents are doctors when their parents retired. I ask for details: Did they go part-time at first, or just retire cold turkey? What are they doing now to fill their days? Do they miss medicine? Do they volunteer? Are they travelling more?

Many of the attending physicians who trained me as a medical student, who seemed old at that time, are still working more than a decade later. Now we are colleagues, peers, so to speak. They walk slowly through the hospital, sometimes assisted by canes. Quite a few have hunches in their backs. None seem particularly happy. My younger colleagues and I sneer at them in hushed conversations: "I'll never work when

I'm that old." I don't think any of these doctors are working out of financial necessity. I think they are working because they're afraid of a time when they won't be doctors. In other words, they're all asking the same question as my father: "What else am I going to do?" Sometimes, when I'm most frustrated with my job, I ask myself the same question.

11 THE BUSINESS OF MEDICINE

Xenia once asked, "When do you think patients stopped trusting doctors?"

I told her I didn't know and asked her to answer her own question. I could have responded, "I'm not entirely sure patients *have* stopped trusting doctors," but that would have sounded naïve or deliberately contrary.

"I think it's when patients realized that medicine is a business," she said matter-of-factly.

The television show *ER* was good public relations for the field of medicine. The doctors worked slavishly while wearing a glamorous version of exhaustion in their faces. In many episodes, the emergency room doctors fought against "the system"—hospital administrators, insurance companies, callous physicians outside of the emergency department—to save their patients. Every patient was given a chance to get better, even if it meant staying in the emergency room for days.

ER almost never referenced money. I can't remember a conversation on the show about how much a test would cost. There was no mention of "throughput," which is a guiding philosophy for most emergency rooms—get the patients in and out of the emergency room as fast as possible so new patients can be seen (and billed). When the show left the hospital and focused on the home lives of the doctors, these doctors were portrayed as part of working class Chicago: they lived in small apartments, took public transportation, and ate at dive restaurants. In truth, emergency rooms are a cash cow for hospitals, and emergency room doctors are some of the highest paid physicians, with average salaries above $250,000 per year.

When I took my current job, I was told by my section chief that, technically, I was expected to bill three times my salary. This was my first job out of training and my first exposure to the dollars and cents of being a doctor. "Don't worry, though," he continued, "because they only use that expectation if they want to fire you."

One of my colleagues, despite working at an academic center, has essentially broken free from the university's salary structure. She rents her office from the university and maintains an academic appointment with university benefits by doing two months of teaching service, but otherwise she essentially functions as a private practitioner. The pay model, she says with a smile, is "eat what you kill."

The dollar amount I've billed and the dollar amount my hospital has collected are the two main metrics by which my outpatient practice is evaluated on a biannual basis. In my own evaluation, though, the primary metric I consider is how many patients I have hospitalized. I take pride in keeping my patients out of the hospital.

Medicine is a business, even if we try to keep that part of the equation hidden. The American Medical Association, for example, claims in its official statement, "Since 1847, the American Medical Association has promoted scientific advancement, improved public health, and invested in the doctor and patient relationship."[1] In truth, the AMA is a trade union, and like any union, its goal is to protect its dues-paying members. The AMA counts approximately one-third of the doctors in the United States as members. The AMA represents and fights for the interests of one-third of the doctors in the United States.

This representation, in the 1950s and 1960s, involved a campaign against Medicare. In the 1990s, this representation helped defeat Bill Clinton's attempts at health care reform, and this same representation fought hard to soften the potential blow (against its members) of Barack Obama's Affordable Care Act. The AMA has one of the largest lobbying budgets of any organization in the United States. Studies done by the Center for Responsive Politics and published on their website, opensecrets.org, revealed that the AMA was the second largest lobbying group in Washington between 1998 and 2011, trailing only the Chamber of Commerce.[2]

Most professions have unions who advocate for their members. The AMA's advocacy does not extend to patients and, at times, even appears to be at the expense of patients. For this reason, most doctors shy away from talking about the "business of medicine."

When I started medical school, I wanted to be a rural doctor. Some of this was due to romanticism. I had a crush on a girl in college who also wanted to be a rural doctor. She went to a different medical school, and I never saw her after college graduation, but I dreamed we'd have a better chance of somehow running into each other again in the future if we were both rural doctors.

I romanticized the idea of the country doctor, beloved by his or her small town, paid with ham by patients who had no money. I envisioned myself as an Atticus Finch-like figure, even though Atticus was a lawyer and not a doctor. William Carlos Williams practiced in a fairly urban section of New Jersey, but I still viewed him as a country doctor based on the way he retold some of his doctoring adventures. I dreamed of living in Vermont or Maine, seeing patients during the day, writing at night and on the weekends.

Every professor in medical school predicted that I'd give up this fantasy. I told them they were wrong. Today, I am a subspecialist at a tertiary care center in Manhattan. I don't even just specialize in nephrology; I specialize in the rarest forms of kidney disease, a subspecialty within a subspecialty.

My new patient told me he was a funeral home director.

"That must be a hard job," I said. "Having to be around grieving families all the time, you always have to be composed for them, right?"

He was a big man, well over six feet and nearly three hundred pounds, but his voice and his smile were gentle. "It's a vocation," he answered. "Like doctors, it's a calling. Someone wakes you up at three a.m. because her mother just died in hospice and needs your help, you have to want to be there for them. I'm sure it's the same with doctors. You're honored to get that call."

I told him that was a very nice way of putting things, and then we went back to talking about his kidneys.

I constantly remind myself that I'm not a hero. There's a limit to what I can accomplish in a single day, in a week, a month, a year. I arrive at work within a ten-minute range each morning, and I leave each evening within another ten-minute range. This approach to my profession, I concede, is just another version of "the business of medicine." For me, doctoring is a job; for my father, doctoring is a calling. Being a doctor is his lifestyle, his personality. I don't expect to go out to dinner and interact with patients at another table. There are kidneys and lives that I cannot save. At least once per clinic day, I tell a patient his or her kidneys are failing, and there's nothing I can do to stop the failure.

I don't think my father processed such limitations when he was in his prime years of practicing medicine. I think he arrived at work each morning and told himself he would not go home until every sick child who needed him was set on a path toward getting better (even if that path was often just reassurance of a child's parents). I think my father considered his work heroic but didn't view himself, necessarily, as a hero, which is fine, because his patients did, and his wife did, and his children did. Perhaps it's because I'm married to a doctor, but my wife has never expressed any awe or wonder with my work (to be fair, I've never expressed any awe or wonder with her work, either). Juno holds up both of us as heroes and says she wants to be a doctor, but I fear she'll outgrow this wonder just like she'll outgrow shows like *Doc McStuffins*.

I've veered sharply away from the country-doctor-getting-paid-in-ham archetype, and I'd probably tell a medical student with a rural medicine dream to abandon it, much the way I was encouraged to give up mine. That kind of advice, too, falls under the heading of "the business of medicine." I've become comfortable being the modern version of a doctor, hyper-specialized, paid with insurance and Medicare dollars. Just doing my job.

12 A DIAGNOSIS (SOMETHING TO DO)

At Mateo's four-month appointment, Dr. Owens told us she was confused. "I can't figure out why he's still having blood in his stools. In my experience, it always goes away when moms cut out dairy and soy." He was growing and gaining weight and was a happy baby, she noted, "so whatever this turns out to be, it probably won't be significant or permanent."

I was hyperaware of how she was now choosing words. She was no longer talking to us as physician colleagues, or even as the son and daughter-in-law of her partner. She was speaking to us as patients, and this kind of language unsettled me. "At this point," Dr. Owens eventually said, "I think we should ask for some help from a specialist."

After the appointment, in our car, Xenia said, "I feel guilty, like we did the wrong thing. Maybe I shouldn't have cut out milk. Maybe I shouldn't have cut out soy. Maybe we should have just forced him to adapt to those foods. Now he has to see an allergist, and I don't want him to be this ultra-sensitive kid." I reminded her how fussy Mateo had been before she cut out milk, and how happy he seemed now. I reminded her that Dr. Owens said this thing, whatever it was, probably would go away on its own. "In Mexico, there's no way they're asking moms to get rid of milk and soy and gluten," Xenia countered. "And the kids there turn out fine." I told her Mateo would be fine. "Why does every kid in America need a diagnosis?" she responded.

On the phone that night with her mother, Xenia said that we'd created this problem for Mateo. At least, I think that's what she said. I could only hear her end of the conversation, and she was flipping back and forth between English and Spanish. I was doing the dishes while she talked to her mother in the next room. I think she said to her mother, "He probably would have gotten through this on his own. Do you know of anyone in our family who's allergic to anything?" I think she responded to whatever her mother said, "Exactly, because parents in Mexico aren't obsessed with everything that goes in and comes out of their kids."

My father, on his own, ran Mateo's case by a pediatric gastroenterologist. "She said it's fine for you guys to start with an allergist," he said. I didn't like the word "start" in that sentence. "I don't want him to see GI," I told my father. "I don't want him to get scoped." I was relieved when Dr. Owens had suggested we take Mateo to an allergist. I'd feared she was going to suggest a gastroenterologist, in which case an endoscopy and/or colonoscopy seemed predestined. My father and I were talking on the phone. He told me not to worry. His voice was calm. He was speaking slowly and hardly stuttering. He was using his talking-to-patients voice with me and employing the techniques he's worked on, for years, with a speech therapist. He said he didn't think Mateo would need any procedures. Like Dr. Owens, he thought this would all pass. "No one knows what to think about occult blood in an asymptomatic infant," he said, "because no one consistently checks it." Unless the parents are two physicians who bring home stool cards from work.

The allergist suggested that Xenia continue to stay off dairy and soy and, in addition, cut out eggs from her diet. He also recommended that we try to expose Mateo to farm animals. He told Xenia that a trip to the zoo was good, but a weekend or weeklong stay at a working farm would be much better. He couldn't give her a precise mechanism or scientific rationale for why this maneuver seemed to work with allergic children other than the well-known hygiene hypothesis of building up a child's immune system with early exposure to antigens. "At least it gives us something to do," Xenia said that night as she began searching online for farm stays within driving distance.

Thanks to the allergist, we now had a name for what Mateo was dealing with: food protein-induced enterocolitis syndrome, or FPIES. Xenia showed me the notes she'd taken during Mateo's appointment. Her frantic handwriting, the way she triple underlined FPIES, reminded me of the way my own patients try to transcribe what I tell them. "Don't worry about writing everything down," I always tell them. "I'll send you a copy of my note. And I can print out a patient handout from the web about the things we're talking about." They always keep writing, though. It gives them something to do.

While Xenia searched for farms, I searched for information on FPIES. I wanted to read about the syndrome in the medical literature, but the first result that came up on my Google search was the FPIES Foundation's website. I was hesitant to explore the site, not wanting to buy into the "my child is sick" narrative, because Mateo looked and acted completely healthy. I thought about a recent patient, a college freshman who'd just been diagnosed with polycystic kidney disease. His mother, a few hours after his first appointment, emailed me to ask if I knew of a polycystic kidney disease foundation for which she could run a fundraising half or full marathon.

If I read about FPIES in a medical journal, I could ascribe the reading to intellectual curiosity and continuing education. I didn't want to be the patient or the patient's father. I wanted to approach this issue from an objective doctor's point of view: stop checking the stools for blood, appreciate the health and happiness of your son, and don't try to rush a resolution. "This thing will declare itself as more serious or completely harmless within a few months," I could picture myself saying to a patient, using my Don Draper voice.

The FPIES Foundation's homepage displayed pale-looking kids forcing a smile for the camera. There were links to read about the importance of food journals, inspirational family stories, and FPIES in the news. The site hosted an online support forum for families to introduce themselves and tell their FPIES stories. I closed the browser.

13 EVERYTHING YOU SAY IS IMPORTANT TO ME

I asked a colleague if she could recommend a colorectal surgeon for a patient of mine, and she gave me a name. Then she said, "He's great. He's really smart, and he really cares about his patients." This was such a natural way for one doctor to praise another, an implicit admission that there are many doctors who are not smart, and many who don't care about their patients. Doctors' language is loaded with subtext. When we talk to each other, we assume the subtext is understood.

When we talk to patients, we can wield this subtext like a weapon. It's easy to offer a therapy to a patient when it has a high likelihood of success; it's far more difficult to embark upon a treatment course when the prospect of failure exists. Communication throughout either of these processes is crucial, of course, but much more so in the latter arena, which is where so many complicated diseases fall. Thus, the art of treating such diseases rests heavily on how data are presented to patients and how prognoses are conveyed. Daniel Kahneman and Amos Tversky, psychologists who developed the prospect theory of behavioral economics, have shown that people's attitudes toward risks concerning gains are usually quite different from their attitudes toward risks concerning losses.[1] Their theories hold true in my instinctive approach to risk/benefit discussions. When I recommend a drug to patients, I tell them it has a 65 percent success rate in clinical trials. When I discuss the drug's side effect profile, I tell them 85 percent of patients don't experience any significant reactions. If I didn't want the patient to take the drug, I'd say, "Unfortunately, 1 in 3 patients won't see any benefit with therapy, and about 1 in 6 will suffer a serious side effect." The conversation is entirely different.

A study at MD Anderson Cancer Center asked patients with a diagnosis of advanced cancer to watch one of two videos (the video assignment was random). Each video showed a professional actor, portraying a physician, discussing treatment and prognostic information with another professional actor, portraying a patient with advanced cancer who had received several lines of chemotherapy, had poor performance status, and was not a good candidate for additional therapy. In one video, the physician provided explicit information about the lack of further treatment options (video A: less optimistic). In the other video, the physician added vague information about possible future treatments, including a statement considering the possibility of further treatments if the patient improved in functional status (video B: more optimistic). The actors deliberately acted the same way in each video, with the same body language and delivery of both messages. After watching the videos, the MD Anderson patients were asked to rate the physicians' compassion and professional performance. The physician-actors from video B (more optimistic message) scored significantly higher compassion and trustworthiness scores than the physician-actors from video A (less optimistic message).[2] One interpretation of this study is that higher perception of compassion is associated with greater trust in the medical profession. Another interpretation is that physicians may be reluctant to give bad news because they don't want to be seen as uncompassionate and untrustworthy.

I showed this study to Xenia, the ultimate straight-shooter, hoping she'd share my frustration at its findings. Instead, she said the results depressed her. Eventually, she spent an entire session with her therapist talking about how the study made her question if she was a bad doctor. I asked her what they talked about. "About how it made me feel like patients and their families want us to blow smoke up their butts and give them false hopes. I've always thought the way I talk to patients and their families—the way I ground them, give them realistic expectations, help them understand how bleak things are—I've always thought that's what distinguishes me, because that kind of honest communication takes so much more time than just loading them up with false hopes." I asked her why this depressed her rather than frustrated her. "Because all this time I've been telling myself that I'm doing the right thing," she answered, "but maybe it's the wrong thing. Maybe I'd be a better doctor if I were more optimistic. Maybe my patients would do better if I had more hope. But the problem is I can't be more optimistic about the patients I see. We send them out of the hospital and know it's just a matter of time before they come right back for the same exact reason."

I commiserated with Xenia and said I was an equally bad doctor. But I didn't mean what I said. I think what she does is admirable. I consider delivering bad news a skill only the best doctors possess. It's so much easier to be positive than to be negative. After this conversation with Xenia, though, I listened to myself talking to patients, face-to-face or over the phone. I critiqued the way I relayed bad results and poor prognoses, and I realized I couldn't help but blow a little smoke up my patients' butts, as Xenia would say. "Look, before you get too upset about these labs, let's repeat them in two or three weeks to make sure they're accurate and not just an outlier," I'd say, and the patients ate it up. On the rare occasion a patient questioned the smoke I was blowing, I wouldn't continue the charade. If a patient asked, for example, "What are the chances that these labs aren't accurate," I'd answer, "Very low. They're almost always accurate."

But most of the time the patients didn't question my optimism. Like me, they probably didn't even recognize my words as false optimism. They probably considered me a compassionate and trustworthy doctor, someone who still hopes they will get better. They'd probably reject Xenia and her stick-to-the-facts-even-when-they're-grim philosophy and come to someone like me for a second opinion. I'd be their hero, Xenia would be their villain, and I'd enjoy playing the heroic role despite knowing that Xenia was doing the better and harder job.

Patients hang on their doctors' words. A patient asked me if she was cured. She wanted me to say yes. Instead, I told her, "We never say cure. We say remission. Your disease is in remission. It could always come back." Sure enough, her disease relapsed two years later. "You responded before, so you should respond again," I counseled her. "I have every reason to think we'll get you back into remission." I've stolen the lexicon of oncologists. These terminologies cushion blows, dampen expectations, and, to some extent, force the patient to never lose contact with his or her doctor.

"Everything you say," another patient said, "is important to me." He was in his late sixties and, originally from Poland, spoke English in choppy sentences that were so loud they verged upon shouts. I'd just told him that his labs were good. His newly transplanted kidney was functioning well. "I remember, I used to wake up in the night and cry," he roared, "because you said the kidney wasn't working." He started to laugh. "Last year, you said, 'Kidney no good,' and I woke up at night and cried. Isn't that funny? I was crying about my kidney." He was still laughing, and I felt obliged to return the laugh.

A patient, seeing me for a third opinion, criticized the previous two physicians who'd cared for him: "I just wish sometimes a doctor would just come out and say, 'I don't know.' I'd at least respect him for his honesty." I say "I don't know" to patients, but I need to follow that confession with at least three or four hypotheses. "I don't know exactly what's going on," I'll say, "but I have a few theories I'd like to explain, and I think there's a chance one or more of those explanations will turn out to be the answer." If I said "I don't know" without the addendum, I suspect my patients would lose confidence in me.

When I deliver a poor prognosis—for example, when I tell patients they'll be in kidney failure and require dialysis or a transplant within the next year—I always add a disclaimer. "That's my prediction. I could be wrong. I hope I'm wrong. I love being wrong in these kinds of situations. But, in all honesty, I don't expect to be wrong in this situation." These patients walk beneath a banner proclaiming my hospital's slogan—"Amazing Things Are Happening Here"—each time they visit my office. Often, as they're leaving the office, I offer my own version of a tagline: "We'll plan for the worst and hope for the best."

14 HARP LIES

I first heard the phrase "harp lie" on Starlee Kine's tragically short-lived podcast, *Mystery Show*. "If I tell you I'm a great piano player or a great singer, you can pretty easily figure out if I'm lying," Kine explained. "It's easy to find a piano, even easier to just ask me to sing something. But if I tell you I'm a great harp player, what are the chances you'll be able to find a harp to see if I'm telling the truth? So I call those kinds of lies, the ones that you can never prove one way or the other, 'harp lies.'"[1] Am I the only doctor who'd hear such a thing on a podcast and reflexively think of talking to patients, answering some of their ridiculous questions with my own version of a "harp lie"?

There's no definitive way to test babies for allergies, so FPIES is a clinical diagnosis. There's a degree of trust that parents must have in their doctors, who say don't eat this and don't eat that. The diagnosis of FPIES, on the one hand, is a paradigm of the old-fashioned version of medicine for which I praise physicians like my father: a doctor takes a history, examines the patient, does no further testing, and makes a diagnosis complete with recommendations. On the other hand, are such versions of medicine old-fashioned because they are examples of harp lies? Can we blame patients, who demand expensive testing and second opinions rather than accepting their doctors' advice without question, for wanting to be certain they're not hearing harp lies?

At dinner, my father told Xenia, after she declined dessert, "You can probably eat a little bit of dairy here and there, a little bit of soy. Eggs once a week. I don't think you need to be totally abstinent."

Later that night, Xenia told me how much my father had upset her. "He has no idea how hard it's been to avoid those foods. I basically eat nuts and fruit all day long, like a squirrel." I told her she was right. He had no idea of the sacrifices she was making. He was just trying to offer her an easier path than the one she'd chosen. "If I'm going to do it," Xenia continued, "I'm not going to do it half-assed. Imagine how you'd feel if something you ate directly hurt your child. Would you eat it?"

I answered, "I think what he was trying to say, though, is that it may be a threshold thing, that if you just have a little bit of those foods, it's not going to hurt Mateo."

She rolled onto her side, turning her face away from me, addressing our bedroom walls. "How, exactly, does he know that?"

Bernard Lown, in *The Lost Art of Healing*, confesses, "At times I have gone so far as to guarantee recovery when the scientific basis for a cure was tenuous or nonexistent.

What is at stake in promising a cure that does not follow? The doctor may be proved wrong and possibly lose the patient's confidence or invite a malpractice suit. However, my many years of medical practice have convinced me that if a patient perceives that the doctor is motivated exclusively by concern for his or her well-being, the patient's trust is rarely diminished, even when the doctor turns out to have been wrong. On a number of occasions when I promised a cure that did not come about, the patients were almost apologetic, as though they had failed me by not living up to my expectations."[2] Some doctors might call this bluffing. Others would consider this a version of the placebo effect. Patients, though, would probably read Lown's confession as a variant of harp lying.

But what, exactly, is wrong with harp lying if it's done with the intention of making a patient feel better? Especially if it works? This is not medical hocus-pocus, according to Lown, who ritually put his hand on every patient's shoulder at the end of an appointment and said, "You'll be fine." He'd seen his own mentors do the same thing and watched their patients "be fine" despite grim diagnoses. The most refreshing part of Lown's memoir is his optimism about what a doctor can do for his or her patients simply by taking a genuine interest in their well-being, even if there's no medicine or science behind that interest.

Lown doesn't use the word placebo, but he's dancing around the well-known placebo effect that exists in doctor-patient relationships. The "improved performance that some individuals experience when they receive what appears to be appropriate help, that may actually be specious, for the situation they are in"—the definition of placebo effect provided by the excellent anthology *Placebo Talks: Modern Perspectives on Placebos in Society*—is the ultimate example of how doctors can effectively bluff (or harp lie) their way to good outcomes. Most of the authors in *Placebo Talks* replace the term "placebo effects" with more specific language, such as "context effects," "meaning effects," and "care effects." This last idea—the care effect—could serve as a tidy encapsulation of Lown's art of healing. Physicians, according to Natasha Campbell and Amir Raz, serve as "walking placebos" with their "ability to change expectancy, experience, and outcome by capitalizing on certain conditioned social cues and choosing words wisely, in order to create an optimal healing environment."[3]

I realize that many of these ideas and concepts come perilously close to paternalism, a taboo subject in modern medicine, where phrases like "Doctor knows best" or "Trust me, I'm a doctor" are reserved for ironic T-shirts. What's fascinating about Lown's memoir and, even more so about the various entries in *Placebo Talks*, is that these authors openly embrace a certain type of paternalism. In fact, more than one placebo expert uses the analogy of a parent kissing "better" a child's boo-boo to explain the expectancy effect of a successful placebo therapy. The ethicist Bennett Foddy has argued that the placebo effect, deployed when a doctor expresses genuine concern for a patient, "involves a special case of deception, which is not subject to the same ethical objections as other forms of clinical deception,"[4] provided that the doctor's goals in deceiving the patient are shared by the patient.

So how does a doctor, like me, know what a patient wants? The poet Claudia Rankine, in *Don't Let Me Be Lonely*, defines loneliness as "what we can't do for each other."[5] I suspect that patients don't want their doctors to let them feel that version of loneliness. Patients want their doctors always working toward some helpful intervention that reaches across the loneliness abyss separating the sick from the healer, even if this intervention is nothing more than an expression of empathy. Like every parent, I'm sure, my knee-jerk reaction whenever Juno falls and starts crying is to pick her up and offer to kiss her better. She always says yes to my offer, and so often that kiss alone is enough to alleviate her pain. It's as if Juno's reaction to my kiss is a deep-felt desire to believe there's nothing we can't do for each other.

Relaying Mateo's diagnosis to my older brother, Xenia included an anecdote about her co-worker, Anjali, whose son had similar symptoms. "Then, as luck would have it, they went to India for a month for a family wedding, and they stayed with her family in a relatively rural area, and by the time they came back to America, her son was completely cured." My brother joked, "Essentially, you have the ultimate first world problem."

The first farm we stayed at was in a Western part of New York I'd never before even looked at on a map. We stopped in a town seven miles away to load up on food for the weekend, as the farmer's wife had told me on the phone that the only food she'd provide us was "as many eggs as you and your family can get out of the chicken coop." We bought locally grown spinach, locally processed sausage, locally caught trout, locally picked apples, and locally made pasta. We filled a growler with dark ale from a nearby brewery. Despite being dairy-free, soy-free, and egg-free, we were not exactly roughing it with food.

When we arrived on the farm, we were greeted by the farmer and his sheep dog, who immediately fell into a game of fetch with Juno using a pine cone. Xenia and I brought our bags and food inside, and I set up the Pack-n-Play for Mateo's crib while she nursed him. It was nearing his bedtime, so while Xenia put Mateo to sleep, I took Juno for a walk around the farm to scope out the animals. The farmer invited us into the stables to see three baby goats, born just an hour before our own arrival at the farm. He wasn't the least bit interested in hearing about Mateo's allergies and the science behind bringing an infant to his farm. He cradled the smallest goat in his arms and kissed its head. "You'll be giving this one a bottle tomorrow," the farmer instructed Juno, who was hiding shyly behind my legs.

The farm had limited cell phone service, so Xenia had to walk up the road to get a signal that night. When she returned to the guesthouse, she said, "I think I saw a *burro*."

"Why would they have a donkey up here?" I asked in disbelief. "You probably just saw an ugly sheep, and it's dark."

"I'm pretty sure it was a *burro*," she insisted. "I really like this place—it reminds me of Divis." Divis is short for Divisaderos, the small town in Mexico where her mother's family is from and where some of her uncles, to this day, work as cattle ranchers. "You and Juno already smell like my Tio Martin."

The next day, Juno gave the smallest baby goat a bottle of formula. She helped stack the hay for all the goats and sheep to eat for breakfast. She gave grain to the chickens and turkeys. She gathered our breakfast out of the chicken coop. In the afternoon, she brushed down one of the farmer's five horses. Xenia and I took turns carrying Mateo in his Baby Bjorn, facing out so he could touch all the animals and then put his fingers in his mouth. "Are you a *granjero*?" Juno asked him. "Are you feeling better, baby?" We took pictures standing next to Arlo, the farm's donkey.

After the farm visit, we stopped checking Mateo's stools for blood on a daily basis. We spaced out the tests to every week. When we realized how much better we felt not having to see the positive stool cards each night, we backed the tests up to every two weeks.

I should say that no one would have ever known something was wrong with Mateo. When he started daycare, we didn't tell the teachers anything about his potential allergies, as we were the ones providing his food. Then, on a Sunday, a few weeks after that first farm visit, Xenia noticed a large amount of mucous in his stool for the first time in weeks. On Monday,

I asked the daycare teachers to save all of his poopy diapers for us in a plastic bag so we could check them for blood. They looked at me as if I was insane.

"Daddy," Juno said, "how do you say *vitaminas* in English?"

"Vitamins," I said.

"Maybe Mateo just needs vitamins," she advised.

I was carrying a Ziploc freezer bag stuffed with Mateo's dirty diapers when she made this suggestion.

15 THE LONGER YOU STAY, THE LONGER YOU STAY

"I don't want any of my kids to become doctors," I told my sister-in-law. "I don't think it's a very happy professional life, and I don't see the job becoming any happier in the future." We were talking about my nephew, her son, who was just beginning his college application process. She told me that her father had pushed her to be either premed or prelaw when she'd started college. He'd told her a medical or law degree was useful. She'd always have a job. She'd always be able to use her degree for something. Growing up, if someone asked her what she wanted to be, she'd answer a pediatrician. She dropped premed after one semester, went on to study economics and communications, and took a job as a publicist for a movie studio. She's now a full-time mother of four. We had this conversation just a few days after Xenia had returned to work. She'd taken off three months to be with

Mateo, and in that last month, she'd tell me nearly every night how much she dreaded going back to work.

"Well," my sister-in-law said, "your father has ten grandchildren, and there could still be one or two more. I just hope that at least one of them goes into medicine. We need to have doctors in the family." Later, after the conversation had already shifted to another subject, she said, "Wait, are you saying you don't like your job?"

I took a moment to figure out her question as we'd just been discussing potential Mother's Day gifts. "No, I do, some days," I said. "It's just that the job is harder than it needs to be, and it's the kind of job I wouldn't wish on my kids. I want them to do something more enjoyable. I want them to wake up every morning eager to go to work. Most doctors don't feel that way."

"Your dad still does," she says.

"He did," I corrected her. "I'm not sure he still does. The job's not what it used to be. Even for him."

She looked upset. Doctors rarely bemoan the profession to nondoctors, because they are patients and shouldn't have to think about the job satisfaction of their doctors. In contrast, doctors crap on the profession to other doctors all the time. My ophthalmologist, after asking me where I'd gone to school, told me that both his children had graduated from Harvard, too. "Medical school?" I asked. "No, college," he said. "Are you kidding? They wanted nothing to do with medicine after seeing how hard I worked. Can you blame them?"

Physician burnout is a big problem. According to a recent study from the Mayo Clinic, 54.4 percent of physicians admitted to at least one symptom of burnout in a survey sent to over 35,000 doctors (one of the signs of burnout, not directly commented upon in the study, is that only 6,880 doctors filled out the survey).[1] Sometimes burnout shows up in obvious ways, like doctors leaving clinical practice for jobs with insurance companies or pharmaceutical companies. Sometimes burnout is subtler. On Friday afternoons, if I have a patient in the hospital, I send an email to the covering physician for the upcoming weekend. If the patient is doing well, I write, "Keep it that way." If the patient is doing poorly, I write, "Fix him." The unwritten joke, of course, is that either of these things is possible.

If I anticipate that a call into an insurance company for prior authorization of a drug will be lengthy, I'll use a different voice for the entire call. The impression simulates an older, prim-and-proper physician who's just trying to keep his wits while he navigates the insurance company's obstacle course. The impression is the only way I can keep my frustration and anger in check while I navigate the same obstacle course. "Why do you need all this darn information?" I'll ask cluelessly. "Why are you giving me and my patient so much grief?" I'll inquire. "Dagnabbit, I'm just trying to help these sick people and you're making it gosh darn hard to do that, young man!"

Nietzsche's famous line, "He who fights with monsters might take care lest he thereby become a monster," is a perfect appraisal of my phone calls to insurance companies. At times, I'll forego the country bumpkin impressions and spit fire into the phone. I'm no longer talking, and I'm certainly not doctoring. I'm venting. When I realize that the insurance company will not approve a medicine or a diagnostic test, I should save myself time and effort and just get off the phone. But I continue to vent. I take on a new character of a maniac doctor who can't recognize that he's lost. Later, I calmly tell the patient whose plan of care has been denied, "I tried, I tried. You can ask my secretaries—I practically screamed at the insurance company." The patients seem to like that character of a doctor who screamed into the phone on their behalf.

"Even though tomorrow's *Sabado*," I whispered to Juno as I put her down to sleep on Friday night, "Daddy needs to work."

"In the *hospital*? In the *ciudad*?" she asked.

"Yes," I said.

"But I'll see you for the *cena*?" she asked. Her voice was sleepy.

"I hope so," I said.

"But why are they in the *hospital*, Daddy?" she asked. I was already standing in her doorway by this point in our exchange.

"Well, that's Daddy's *trabajo*," I answered, "to figure out why they're sick and in the *hospital*, and then figure out a way to make them better so they can go *a la casa*." In truth,

I spend my weekends on call plugging holes, applying Band-Aids, holding the fort, whatever cliché best describes the process of seeing twenty to thirty patients I don't know and making sure they don't crash until Monday, when the regular, fully staffed team can take over their care.

The next morning, as the on-call weekend nephrologist, I told a young man whose kidneys were failing far more rapidly than the weekday team had predicted that I wanted to start him on dialysis. "It's not an emergency," I said just a few minutes after introducing myself. "Not yet, but if we don't get you started by the end of today, I'm afraid we'll run into an emergency overnight." The patient, through labored breaths, agreed to my plan and said he didn't have any questions. He even forced a smile for me. I don't remember his name, I barely remember his face other than that forced smile, and I don't know a single thing about him other than why his kidneys deteriorated so quickly. Still, I was the person who told him on a rainy Saturday morning that his kidneys had stopped working and a machine was the only way to prevent him from dying of kidney failure. And because I'd said those words so many times before, all I thought about during our brief conversation was that his unexpected decline into kidney failure probably was going to prevent me from having dinner with my family.

An expression I heard throughout training was "the longer you stay, the longer you stay." If you leave the hospital, the nurses will bother some other resident or fellow, but if they see you, they will bother you. I suppose "the longer you stay, the longer you stay" could apply to any kind of job, but I wonder if other professions use the expression.

From my perspective, the closest profession to medicine is police work. Granted, my perspective is entirely based on films and television shows, and primarily influenced by the HBO series, *The Wire*. Assuming *The Wire*'s depiction of police work bears some semblance to reality, though, I see a number of parallels between being a cop and being a doctor. Chief among those similarities is that both doctors and cops have to "eat shit" (a phrase uttered throughout all five seasons of *The Wire*) from their superiors. Both hate paperwork and documentation, in general. Both have no off switch, both have ill-defined hours, both work weekends, both never call in sick, both post higher-than-average rates of substance abuse and divorce and suicide. Both burn out.

One of my favorite lines from *The Wire* is when McNulty says to Bunk, "This'll teach you to give a fuck when it ain't your turn."[2] They're talking about investigating a fresh murder scene, but the warning applies to so much of the policing on *The Wire* and so much of the doctoring in my hospital. It's just another way of saying "the longer you stay, the longer you stay," but the language cuts deeper into the guilt that doctors (and, I presume, cops) feel about experiencing burnout. We're supposed to give a fuck, and we're supposed to give a fuck all the time, not just when it's our turn. But that kind of effort and commitment wears us out.

A study done at a university-based residency program in Seattle, using the Maslach Burnout Inventory, found that 76 percent of the responding residents met their prespecified criteria for burnout. The investigators also asked the residents about patient care practices and attitudes and found that this high degree of burnout translated to residents, for lack of a better phrase, not giving a fuck at an alarming frequency. More than a third agreed with this statement: "At least monthly, I found myself discharging patients to make the service 'manageable' because the team was so busy." Ten percent admitted to not fully discussing treatment options or answering a patient's questions. Twenty percent reported little emotional reaction to a patient's death. And about one in seven residents admitted to feeling guilty about how they treated a patient "from a humanitarian standpoint."[3]

Xenia is the rare doctor who still uses a beeper. Like most doctors, I gave my pager up years ago and use my cell phone as the way for other doctors, nurses, and hospital operators to contact me. Xenia likes to keep her work separate from her home. "I don't want people in the hospital having my cell phone," she explains.

Juno likes to wear her mom's beeper when she's playing dress up and in a doctor mood. "Whoooooooaaah," she says. "It's so heavy." She wears the pager clipped to her purple corduroy pants or the waistband of her rainbow-striped tights, prancing around our living room. She periodically looks down, waiting for the pager to beep. I don't know why

I've never thought to call the beeper while she's wearing it, to let her experience the phenomenon of being paged. Maybe it's because I never felt anything but annoyance or dread when my pager rang. My heart rate rose. My face flushed. Sometimes I'd say "fuck," my own version of my father's "shit." Part of the reason why I like using a cell phone rather than a pager is because the phone's buzz could be anything—Xenia asking about dinner, a friend wanting to catch up, the library telling me a book on hold is ready for pick up—and doesn't automatically imply more work and more responsibility.

Absolving some of this responsibility is necessary for doctors to keep a sane head, but it's still a concession of our limitations. I always make a point of mentioning in my notes when I last saw a patient. "Her last visit with me was three months ago" or "I have not seen him in over a year." This is my way of deflecting any blame for what might have gone wrong in the time between visits, when it wasn't my turn to give a fuck.

If I won the lottery, I'd quit the next day. You always hear these stories about the gas station attendants or the bus drivers or the secretaries who win the lottery but keep working because they love their jobs, so I guess this means I don't love my job. Xenia says I would keep working. She claims I like my job more than I admit. If I'm in a good mood, I concede that I would keep working, but only part-time, and I'd only do the parts of my job that I enjoy. I'd hire a personal assistant to do all of my paperwork.

I am generally happy with my life. Xenia and I argue frequently, but we are still in love with each other. My children are gifts. I look at their pictures on my phone at least a half dozen times each day. I have a nice house. My car is a hybrid. I can walk to my town's public library and community pool and weekly farmers market. I've accepted that most professional sporting outcomes are random, and so the Mets, Jets, and Knicks no longer wreck my days and night. In high school, I thought about using a Nirvana lyric for my yearbook quote: "I miss the comfort in being sad." I chickened out, though, worried what my parents or teachers would think once they read the line. Still, I felt that way then, and I wonder if I feel that way now. Am I uncomfortable being content and, therefore, turned to my job, to medicine, for sadness?

Or is the job of doctoring, over time, unavoidably sad and frustrating? After seeing one of the sickest patients I'd seen in a while, a woman with end-stage Parkinson's disease and impending kidney failure, a woman who was destined to spend her last few months alive in an utterly decrepit condition, I went out to the waiting room to get a glass of water from the water cooler. The patients were all watching a television mounted from the ceiling. They were watching *Ellen*. They were watching Ellen DeGeneres dancing merrily down the stairs, jumping up and down with her studio audience. I finished my water, turned away from the television, and forced a smile as I called in the next patient.

A few days later, Mateo was sitting on my lap, and Juno was performing for both of us in the living room, singing about the five little monkeys jumping on the bed. With each subsequent fall, with each call from the mama to the doctor, her voice rose into an angrier and angrier pitch, so that by the time she got to two little monkeys jumping on the bed, she was practically screaming the doctor's instructions: "No more monkeys jumping on the bed!" Going through the motions of the song—the tedious countdown from five to four to three to two little monkeys—appeared to have frustrated the doctor in the song. The doctor's first instructions had been delivered with a smile, with optimism and a sense of collective hope. We can fix this problem together. Now, the doctor was furious with the mother for ignoring such simple directives. Juno had identified not with the little monkeys, not with the mama, but with the doctor, who turned out to be utterly powerless in the physician-patient relationship.

16 THE FUTURE IS ALREADY HERE

When the Ebola scare took over my hospital, the chairman of medicine asked for volunteers to take care of patients who'd be isolated for suspicion of the virus. All consultations would be done via telemedicine: a camera would be installed in the room, and the interview would be done remotely. No physical exam would be required. No contact would occur. This policy felt like an admission that we could do our jobs without seeing the patients and that, on some level, we were afraid of our patients.

Telemedicine exists in other formats. Patients email their doctors a list of symptoms, a WebMD link to an article about pneumonia, and ask if they should be on antibiotics. Doctors use electronic medical records that automatically generate letters to patients with their lab results and standardized explanations for any values that are outside of normal range. Insurance companies have online portals for patients and physicians to request medication approvals. Smart phone apps house data on blood pressure, heart rate, and glucose levels that can be sent from patient to doctor instantaneously. All the while, opportunities for thoughtful conversations and meaningful encounters disappear.

I understand why medicine needs to keep evolving and advancing, even if this evolution comes at the expense of the doctor-patient relationship. After Xenia and I had been trying to get pregnant for two years, my older brother, an orthopedic surgeon, asked me why we hadn't seen a fertility specialist yet.

"We really want to do this naturally," I said.

"But you may not be able to," he replied. "Our fertility doctor told us there was literally no way we could have a child without help." I asked him if he believed that was true, or just a doctor justifying his work. "Listen," he continued, "50 or 60 years ago, we'd have been one of those couples who just never were able to have kids or who had to adopt. But thanks to modern medicine, we were able to get pregnant. I can't believe I have to explain this to you."

Eventually, Xenia and I did see a fertility doctor, and Juno was almost certainly the result of intrauterine insemination (at our fertility doctor's suggestion, we had sex for two nights after the procedure, so it's at least conceivable that Juno was conceived the old-fashioned way). Three years later, when we wanted to try for another pregnancy, I wrote a prescription for intravaginal progesterone that would allow Xenia to extend her luteal phase. She was pregnant after three months of these home treatments. We never needed to use artificial insemination, but we did have another medically assisted pregnancy.

Thanks to technology, I now have two children, and I can Skype or Facetime with them from my conference hotel room. The last slide of my PowerPoint talk on "Diagnosis and Management of Resistant Hypertension" is a photo of Juno using her toy doctor's kit to check a teddy bear's blood pressure. I can connect Mateo's Motorola baby monitor to my iPhone and watch him sleep while I'm taking the train home from an NIH meeting just outside Washington, D.C. I can tele-parent just as well as I tele-doctor.

Our hospital gives each intern an iPad, ostensibly for work, because they can check labs and look at radiology images using our hospital's medical records app. None do, though. The iPads go home on the first day and rarely surface on the hospital floors. When Xenia runs the teaching service, though, she insists that the interns bring their hospital-issued iPads on rounds. "They groan, because they hate having to carry them around, but it helps on rounds," she says. I should note that Xenia rounds on patients at the bedside instead of in a private conference room; few hospital teams still employ this old-school technique of discussing a case directly in front of the patient. "All the patients—regardless of their age, education, language, background—they all want to see their X-rays and CT scans on the iPad. They're in awe that we can show it to them on a tablet." It makes it look like the doctors control the technology and, consequently, know what they're doing.

In his book, *The Patient Will See You Now*, Dr. Eric Topol foresees a future in which the smartphone will "democratize" medicine by granting patients "unfettered, direct access to all of their own health data and information."[1] Topol argues that technology empowers people to learn as much as possible about their health and alter the dynamics, in a good way, between doctor and patient. When patients control their health information, they have the power to personalize their care—they can see which doctors they want to see, when they want to see them, and even where they want to see them. With a smartphone, he says, "you can have ICU-like monitoring in the safety, reduced expense, and convenience of your home."

If his vision for the future doesn't pan out, Topol says we can blame medical paternalism and doctors who stubbornly hold on to the "doctor knows best" mantra. In an interview about the book, Topol clarified: "I don't believe this technology is replacing doctors at all. This is simply changing the model. Doctors are fully there to review data and provide wisdom, experience, and guidance—not exercise all control."[2]

Topol doesn't clarify that this new model of the technologically savvy, knowledge-is-power patient already exists. In another variant of telemedicine, the wealthiest and most educated patients are already doctor-shopping, medicine-shopping, hospital-shopping, and clinic-shopping before they walk through my clinic doors. As William Gibson said, "The future is already here—it's just not evenly distributed." These patients bring in articles I've written, my paragraphs highlighted in yellow and orange. There's an unspoken message when they show me their preliminary research: you should be honored that I've chosen you as my doctor. And, I'll admit, I am. They are playing to my vanity, and I am a willing accomplice—to a point, at least. At some moment in our encounter, I need to take control of the relationship. I'm okay with eschewing "doctor knows best" in my doctor-patient relationships, but I won't abandon "doctor knows better."

About once a month, my parents babysit so Xenia and I can go out to dinner. We used to call these dinners "date nights" but corrupted that phrase by once using my parents as a means to go grocery shopping, and the idea of a "date night" to Whole Foods seemed depressing. Recently, when we returned from dinner, I found my father staring intently at his iPhone. "Come see this," he said, finally looking up from his screen. He held up his phone, which displayed an EKG strip on the screen. He then showed me two silver clips attached to the back of the phone and, resting his fingers on these clips, demonstrated how he could use the phone to read an instantaneous heart rhythm strip.

"I was having palpitations," he explained, "and saw the new cardiologist at the practice. He's younger than you." My father took another EKG reading and continued. "He said instead of doing a 72-hour home monitor and having to wear one of those annoying machines, I could use this app to monitor my heart rate." I asked him how he downloaded the app, as I'd never seen him download anything on his phone. "The cardiologist did it for me in the office, and he attached the clips for me, too. I see him next week to go over the recordings and return the clips. It's pretty neat, isn't it, that I can do this with my phone?"

My father's face was beaming. He seemed excited to have the kind of medical problem that an iPhone app could evaluate. "You should meet this doctor," he continued. "He reminds me of you." My father's hands shook a bit as he took another EKG recording on his phone. He looked like a patient, like someone who was in awe of a doctor. His admiration of the technology in his hands, of this modern style of doctoring, seemed like a concession that he was on his way out of the field.

"Are you able to read it?" he asked, handing the phone to me.

"It's just normal sinus rhythm," I said, scrolling through the last four or five EKG strips. "They're all just sinus rhythm."

"Well," my father said, taking the phone back, "I'm going to see the doctor next week, and he'll review them, too."

17 HISTORY AND PHYSICAL

We teach the medical students to sit down next to a patient's bed when taking a history. Give the impression that you're not in a rush. Act like the interview is a discussion, a give and take. Start by asking patients why they are in the hospital, and then try not to say anything for at least two minutes.

"When's the last time you felt good?" is a useful question to ask patients. "When's the last time you felt like yourself?" is an equally useful variation. Phrase your questions so that a simple yes or no won't suffice for an answer. Remember, your job is to get the patient to open up and share. Every patient has a tale to tell.

At the end of the interview, always ask the patient: "What do you think is going on? What's your explanation?" A professor told my medical school class, "If you're at the race track, you never ignore a tip from one of the jockeys."

There's a truism in medicine that's not entirely true, but it's important for doctors to think it's true. This truism goes something like, "90 percent of all diagnoses can be made based only on what a patient tells you." I've heard some minor variations of this truism—sometimes the percentage dips to 80 percent; sometimes the 90 percent diagnostic rate requires both the patient's history and physical exam—but the underlying message remains consistent and unwavering. The patients will tell you what's wrong with them if you just pay attention to the stories they are telling.

In academic hospitals, teaching physicians throw around this 90-percent axiom to encourage old-fashioned doctoring skills and make students less reliant on the relatively modern luxuries of lab tests and imaging studies that can be ordered with a click of a mouse. I do believe that most patients can self-diagnose their illnesses (or lack thereof), which is why I still end every patient interview with the "What do you think is going on?" question if the patient hasn't already volunteered his or her own theories.

I believe less and less, however, that the stories patients tell their doctors are accurate reconstructions. The patients, in recounting what doctor notes call "the history of present illness," are picking and choosing the salient elements of their story: the plot points, the clues, the signs and symptoms that would be derided in a fiction workshop as too obvious examples of foreshadowing. The patients are telling a story that ends in the diagnosis they've made on their own. In other words, the patient sitting across the desk from me, answering the question "What brings you to the office today," is real-time drafting a personal essay, and almost certainly doing so without a clear distinction of what's exactly fact and what's a little bit fiction.

When children play doctor with each other, they go right to the physical exam. They listen to the chest with a toy stethoscope, take a blood pressure with a small hand pump, look into the mouth and eyes with a fake light, administer painless shots, and test reflexes with a plastic hammer. The child doctor touches the child patient throughout the exchange. There is almost no talking and, of course, there is no documentation of exam findings. I devote, at most, 10 percent of my time with patients to the physical exam. The rest of the time is spent talking or typing, which is just another way of talking. I have not used a reflex hammer once since my rotation, as a third-year medical student, on the neurology service.

Patients seem to yearn for the child's version of a doctor's visit. Because I specialize in the rarest forms of kidney diseases, most of my new patients are seeking a second or third opinion. In the context of criticizing their previous nephrologists, these patients often tell me that the last doctor didn't even examine them. They may be telling the truth, or they may have simply forgotten a brisk and likely meaningless examination. I often have a fellow or resident shadowing me in clinic. "Well, we examine patients in this office," I say, as much for the patient as for the observing physician-in-training.

Juno, brandishing the plastic otoscope from her doctor's kit, asked me if she could look into my ears.

"*Sí*," I answered.

"Speak English, Daddy," she pleaded.

"*Porque*?" I asked.

"Speak English!" she commanded.

I got down on my knees so she could stick the toy into my ear.

"Looks good, Daddy," she said.

"What were you looking for?" I asked.

"Crumbs," she answered.

For many doctors (myself included), the stethoscope exam has become more ceremony than utility. A colleague, considered one of the best clinicians in the hospital, recently asked me if he could borrow my stethoscope for his clinic. He'd left his in the car. I confessed that I was using an isolation stethoscope, which is a flimsy, disposable, toy-like stethoscope that the hospital stocks for patients who are on isolation for infectious reasons. In fact, this kind of stethoscope is what Juno prefers to use for her own play-doctoring. A doctor could put one end of a paper towel roll against a patient's chest and the other end against his or her ear and get roughly the same level of auscultation as these isolation stethoscopes provide.

"Can I have it?" my colleague asked.

"Sure," I said. "I can just grab another one out of the utility room."

He put the isolation stethoscope around his neck. "Patients expect you to have one of these things," he said before walking away.

During my intern year, I wrote an essay about the dying art of the physical exam that was published in the *New England Journal of Medicine*.[1] I used myself as an example and confessed that my exams, during early morning hospital rounds, were less than thirty seconds. I divulged the secret of the "intern's spot," the magical area on a patient's chest where breath, heart, and bowel sounds can all be heard in record-short time. And I relayed a case of calciphylaxis, a rare complication of kidney failure in which the skin necroses at a rapid and fatal rate. The smell of dying, rotting skin was unforgettable. The intended message of the piece was that as one part of my patient encounter was dwindling (the expected stethoscope exam), another unexpected part was improving (the equally important olfactory exam).

The essay was misinterpreted, though, and has been reprinted in a number of medical school syllabi (including my own) to defend the importance of the stethoscope—and by extension, the full physical exam—to medical students. The stethoscope isn't a tool, anymore, but a metonym for bedside manner.

When Claudia Rankine wrote about "a truce with the patience of a stethoscope,"[2] she couldn't have been thinking of the way my colleagues and I use our stethoscopes. Juno, listening to our four-year-old neighbor's heartbeat with her toy stethoscope, is more patient with her doctoring than any physician I've seen in my hospital. "I can hear it," she says with a smile, her hand cupping our neighbor's chest. "I can hear your heart," she whispers to her friend, as if they've both shared a magical experience.

18 DON'T WORRY

The first farm was great but didn't have any cows, and Mateo's stools still tested positive for occult blood. The allergist recommended we try to stay at a farm with cows. "Owning a cow would be the best therapy," he told Xenia over the phone, "but, since you can't do that, you should try to expose your son to cows as much as possible."

The second farm was cow heaven—close to fifty cows, each with a unique name that made Juno laugh (her favorite was Cray Cray). Twice a day, the cows were brought into a mammoth barn house for milking; once they were hooked up to their pumps, we had free reign to walk around the barn and try to touch them.

We gravitated toward the pregnant cows that were given a break from milking in their last two months of pregnancy. These cows, shuttled into a separate pen, splayed out on a bed of hay and let Mateo and Juno run their hands through their fur.

I held Mateo in my arms and leaned over into the face of an enormous cow, who was in the process of yielding over forty-five pounds of milk (the "milking" was done by electronic pumps, each fitted with a running gauge that ticked off how much milk was produced per session). I took his tiny hand and ran it over the cow's long brow and then let go. He continued to pet the cow, stroking it back and forth, the way he'd touch the furry parts of his touch-and-feel baby books. After a few seconds, I backed away from the cow, so the only thing Mateo could do with his petting hand was thrust it into his mouth, which he dutifully did. The milking barn was composed of stalls for each cow, twelve per lane, and we repeated this action with each of the cows. Four lanes altogether. Forty-eight cows. I approached, saluted each cow by name, and, modeling both good manners and basic Spanish for my son, asked if we could touch her. "*Buenos dias, Beulah. Te podemos tocar?*" I waited a moment, leaned over, and coached Mateo into exposing his hands and his mouth to all of the micro-species that lived within Beulah and the rest of her mates.

I texted a video of Mateo playing with the cows to my older brother. He texted back, "The allergist really recommended that? It seems like he could catch something." I pretended that I was at the appointment, that I was now an expert on infant food allergies. I answered, "He said we should expose him to cows. The more exposure, the better." My brother was skeptical and suggested we run our practices by the allergist. "He may just want him to breathe in some air and not be putting his hands directly from the cow's face into his mouth."

"The cows here look like the cows in Divis," Xenia said. Again, she was referencing the small village in Mexico where her mother had grown up. "This whole place looks like Divis, just a much cleaner version of Divis." She was smiling. We were helping our son with a nature-based therapy. We were picking and choosing from our doctors' assessments of Mateo, opting for an old-fashioned treatment to a very modern diagnosis. No medicines, no procedures, just lifestyle modifications. We were directing his care. We were controlling the narrative of his disease. I wasn't sure if we were reconstructing the story as doctors or as patients, but I liked the version we were telling. Xenia took my hand as we walked from the barn back to the guest cottage where we'd be spending the weekend. I tried to imagine what a photo of us might have looked like—me carrying Mateo in a Baby Bjorn, Xenia holding my hand on one side and Juno's hand on the other side. We would have looked like a perfectly happy family.

That night, we noticed a rash spreading over Mateo's legs and the back of his head. "Do you think it's from the cows?" I asked Xenia. We took turns examining our son. We ran our hands over his naked body, looking for each and every red splotch we could find.

"Maybe it's just heat rash?" Xenia asked.

"It's sort of a weird distribution for that," I countered, pointing out how the rash spared his chest and upper back.

The rash got worse over the weekend, darkening from a light pink to a deeper red, and hardening from a soft lacy texture to something much firmer. Mateo, who was crawling now, didn't seem bothered by his rash. He loved crawling around in the grass. He loved even more standing up with our assistance. He squealed at the cows, goats, sheep, and chickens. We decided against calling our pediatrician. I decided against texting a photo of the rash to my father, something I'd done two summers earlier when Juno broke out in a horrible rash during a Cape Cod vacation. "Looks like hives," my father had texted back in response to a photo of Juno's thighs. "Has she been eating shellfish?" The day before, she'd tried lobster for the first time. At his suggestion, we gave her a small dose of Benadryl; when she woke up from her Benadryl-induced nap, the rash was gone. My father probably could have performed the same diagnostic magic again over text, but I didn't want to run the risk of his failing this time around.

Let's not worry about it, we told ourselves about Mateo's rash. "Maybe this is his body trying to get the allergens out of his system," Xenia said. We held on to this crazy theory for two days. We didn't search Google Images for a match to his rash. We didn't try to make an informed diagnosis by checking reference sites like UpToDate and Medscape. Instead, we doubled down on the idea that going to the farm and being exposed to the cows would cure Mateo. The rash was a physical manifestation of that healing process.

We left the farm on Mother's Day, so we saw my parents that evening. I showed Mateo's legs to my father. The rash was already looking better on its own, but I still wanted his opinion. He examined his grandson, with his granddaughter standing beside him.

"What is it, Bampa?" Juno asked.

"I think it's just a heat rash," my father said, directly addressing Juno. He kissed Mateo on his head and handed him back to Xenia.

"He's going to be okay?" Juno asked my father.

"Absolutely," he said.

"You're sure it's just a heat rash and not something allergic, like a reaction to the cows?" I asked.

"It's a heat rash," he said quickly and confidently, the way a doctor on television would relay a definitive diagnosis. Maybe he was bluffing, although I doubted he'd do that to two physicians, to his son and daughter-in-law. "It'll be gone within a day or two," he continued. "It's just a heat rash. He's going to be fine. Don't worry." He did not seem to be worried himself. In fact, he seemed to be enjoying the moment, savoring the victory of a correct diagnosis. His speech was slow and without the slightest hint of a stutter. He was the kind of doctor he wanted to be, talking the way he wanted to talk, and all that was left was for his patients to accept his words.

Three of her four sons were at Mother's Day dinner, and my mother took the opportunity to speak to each of us alone. "I'm going to push your father to cut back on his schedule, to three days a week," she told me. The week before, they'd gone out to dinner with some of their oldest friends, Mike and Barbara, whom they'd met over forty years ago when my father and Mike (another pediatrician) were stationed at Wright Patterson Air Force Base in Dayton, Ohio. At dinner, Mike told my father he'd cut down to half-time: two and a half days a week with no more weekends. "If Mike can do it, so can your father," my mother said.

I assume she said pretty much the same thing to my older brothers, and I assume they all had the same reaction that I did. My father will resist at first but ultimately acquiesce. Within a year, he will be down to her proposed schedule. And if he thinks he's unhappy with these reduced hours, my mother will figure out a way to convince him that he's not.

Later that night, I caught Juno examining the legs of her doll for rashes. She whispered to the baby doll, "*No te preocupes,*" over and over and over. I stayed silent in her doorway, watching her undress the doll and meticulously inspect every aspect of its body. She was methodical. She was gentle. She was caring. I could have spied on her forever, but she turned around while putting the doll's lilac dress back on and saw me. She blushed.

"It's just a heat rash," she said. Then, with a comforting smile that reminded me of her grandfather's, she added, "Don't worry, Daddy."

ACKNOWLEDGMENTS

Thank you to the editors of the following publications, where portions of this book first appeared, often in significantly different formats: *The Atlantic* ("Why Doctors Still Need Stethoscopes"), *Big Truths* ("The Future Is Already Here"), *Kenyon Review* ("What Do You Do to the *Enfermos*?"), *Los Angeles Review of Books* ("Don't Let Me Be Lonely, Doctor"), *The Millions* ("What Do You Think Is Going On?"), *New Delta Review* ("The Fourth Wall"), and *Ohio Edit* ("Doctor Jokes" and "Role Playing").

Thank you to the earliest readers of this book—Chloe Caldwell, Amy Fusselman, Julie Barer, and Sarah McCann—for the time and thought you gave to a far-from-finished manuscript. Even more, thank you for treating me as a writer-who-doctors rather than a doctor-who-writes.

Thank you to Matt McGowan for sage advice throughout this endeavor.

Thank you to Christopher Schaberg, Ian Bogost, and Haaris Naqvi for welcoming me into the *Object Lessons* family and shepherding this book into existence. I'm honored to be a part of this series.

Thank you to all the doctors and patients who have shared their stories with me since my first day of medical school.

Thank you to Ariadne, Juno, Mateo, and Joaquin for being the loves of my life.

Thank you to Xenia for being my everything.

NOTES

Chapter 1

1 J. Grumet, "Are We Witnessing the Death of the Modern Day Physician?" *The Medical Bag*, December 29, 2014, www.themedicalbag.com/doctor-blogs/jordan-grumet/are-we-witnessing-the-death-of-the-modern-day-physician.

2 D. K. Gjerdingen et al., "Patients' and Physicians' Attitudes Regarding the Physician's Professional Appearance," *Archives of Internal Medicine* 147, no. 7 (July 1987): 1209–12.

Chapter 2

1 T. C. Hoffman and C. Del Mar, "Patients' Expectations of the Benefits and Harms of Treatments, Screening, and Tests: A Systematic Review," *JAMA Internal Medicine* 175, no. 2 (February 2015): 274–86.

2 D. Korenstein, "Patient Perception of Benefits and Harms: The Achilles Heel of High-value Care," *JAMA Internal Medicine* 175, no. 2 (February 2015): 287–8.

3 E. Allen, "Fury Entered Here," *The Boston Globe*, March 8, 2015.

4 S. Tisdale, "Twitchy," *Antioch Review*, Spring 2008.

5 D. Bellamy, *When the Sick Rule the World*, Semiotext(e), 2015.

Chapter 3

1 M. Gladwell, "The Engineer's Lament," *The New Yorker*, May 4, 2015.

Chapter 4

1 B. Lown, *The Lost Art of Healing* (Boston: Houghton Mifflin, 1996).

2 Dr. 99, "Hospitals Unleash New, Brutally Honest Slogans," *Gomer Blog*, January 7, 2015, gomerblog.com/2015/01/hospitals-slogan.

Chapter 6

1 L. Silverman, "Millennial Doctors May Be More Tech-Savvy, But Is That Better?" *National Public Radio*, November 27, 2014, www.npr.org/sections/health-shots/2014/11/27/366766639mill enial-doctors-may-be-more-tech-savvy-but-is-that-better.

2 K. C. Chretien et al., "Physicians on Twitter," *Journal of the American Medical Association* 30, no. 6 (February 2011): 566–8.

3 K. B. O'Reilly, "Anonymous Posts: Liberating or Unprofessional?" *American Medical News*, July 11, 2011.

Chapter 8

1 C. Maraldo, "Concierge Medicine—Medicine the Way it Used to be?" *Examiner.com*, September 6, 2012, www.examiner.com/article/concierge-medicine-medicine-the-way-it-used-to-be.

2 J. Wieczner, "Pros and Cons of Concierge Medicine," *The Wall Street Journal*, November 10, 2013.

3 D. Von Drehle, "Medicine Is About to Get Personal," *Time*, December 22, 2014.

Chapter 10

1 P. Phillips, *Boy* (Athens: University of Georgia Press, 2008).

Chapter 11

1 American Medical Association, "AMA History," www.ama-assn.org/ama-history.

2 Annual lobbying totals by the American Medical Association are available at www.opensecrets.org/lobby/clientsum.php?id=D000000068.

Chapter 13

1 D. Kahneman and A. Tversky, *Choices, Values, and Frames* (Cambridge, UK: Cambridge University Press, 2000).

2 K. Tanco et al., "Patient Perception of Physician Compassion After a More Optimistic vs a Less Optimistic Message: A Randomized Clinical Trial," *JAMA Oncology* 1, no. 2 (May 2015): 176–83.

Chapter 14

1 S. Kine, "Case #1: Video Store," *Mystery Show*, podcast audio, May 21, 2015. gimletmedia.com/episode/1-video-store.

2 B. Lown, *The Lost Art of Healing* (Boston: Houghton Mifflin, 1996).

3 N. Campbell and A. Raz, "Placebo Science in Medical Education," in *Placebo Talks: Modern Perspectives on Placebos in Society*, eds. A. Raz and C. Harris (New York: Oxford University Press, 2016).

4 B. Foddy, "Justifying Deceptive Placebos," in *Placebo Talks: Modern Perspectives on Placebos in Society*, eds. A. Raz and C. Harris (New York: Oxford University Press, 2016).

5 C. Rankine, *Don't Let Me Be Lonely* (Minneapolis: Graywolf Press, 2004).

Chapter 15

1 T. D. Shanafelt et al., "Changes in Burnout and Satisfaction with Work-life Balance in Physicians and the General US Working Population between 2011 and 2014," *Mayo Clinic Proceedings* 90, no. 12 (December 2015): 1600–13.

2 D. Simon, "The Target," *The Wire*, television program, June 2, 2002, HBO.

3 T. D. Shanafelt et al., "Burnout and Self-reported Patient Care in an Internal Medicine Residency Program," *Annals of Internal Medicine* 136, no. 5 (March 2002): 358–67.

Chapter 16

1 E. Topol, *The Patient Will See You Now* (New York: Basic Books, 2015).

2 C. Shortsleeve, "Can Technology Replace Doctors?" *Furthermore*, February 18, 2015, furthermore.equinox.com/articles/2015/02/can-technology-replace-doctors.

Chapter 17

1 A. S. Bomback, "The Physical Exam and the Sense of Smell," *New England Journal of Medicine* 354 (January 2006): 327–9.

2 C. Rankine, *Citizen* (Minneapolis: Graywolf Press, 2014).

INDEX